T0384069

Leading Continuous Improvement Projects

Lessons from Successful, Less Successful, and Unsuccessful Continuous Improvement Case Studies

by

Fernando González Aleu and
Jose Arturo Garza-Reyes

CRC Press
Taylor & Francis Group
Boca Raton London New York

CRC Press is an imprint of the
Taylor & Francis Group, an **informa** business

A PRODUCTIVITY PRESS BOOK

First edition published in 2020
by Routledge/Productivity Press
52 Vanderbilt Avenue, 11th Floor New York, NY 10017
2 Park Square, Milton Park, Abingdon, Oxon OX14 4RN, UK

Routledge/Productivity Press is an imprint of Taylor & Francis Group, an informa business

No claim to original U.S. Government works

Printed on acid-free paper

International Standard Book Number-13: 978-0-367-27167-1 (Hardback)
International Standard Book Number-13: 978-0-429-29577-5 (eBook)

Library of Congress Cataloging-in-Publication Data

Names: Aleu, Fernando González, author. | Garza-Reyes, Jose Arturo, author.
Title: Leading continuous improvement projects : lessons from successful,
less successful, and unsuccessful continuous improvement case studies /
Fernando González Aleu, Jose Arturo Garza-Reyes.
Description: 1 Edition. | New York : Routledge, 2020. | Includes
bibliographical references and index.
Identifiers: LCCN 2019047273 (print) | LCCN 2019047274 (ebook) |
ISBN 9780367271671 (hardback) | ISBN 9780429295775 (ebook)
Subjects: LCSH: Leadership. | Project management.
Classification: LCC HD57.7 .A4174 2020 (print) |
LCC HD57.7 (ebook) | DDC 658.4/092–dc23
LC record available at https://lccn.loc.gov/2019047273
LC ebook record available at https://lccn.loc.gov/2019047274

Visit the Taylor & Francis Web site at
http://www.taylorandfrancis.com

We dedicate this work to our families, whose love, constant

and unconditional support have served as source of

inspiration and strength to complete this book project.

Fernando González Aleu

Jose Arturo Garza-Reyes

Contents

Preface.. xi
Acknowledgements xiii
About the Authors..xv
Introduction xvii

PART I   Continuous Improvement
Projects and Success Factors

Chapter 1   Continuous Improvement Projects (CIPs)
Overview.. 3

    1.1   Introduction 3
    1.2   What is a CIP?..3
    1.3   Types of CIPs...4
    1.4   What Is a Successful CIP? 5
    1.5   Factors Related to CIP Success 6
    1.6   Conclusions 19
    1.7   References 19

Chapter 2   Managing CIPs.. 23

    2.1   Introduction 23
    2.2   Senior Project Inexhaustible Source of CIPs 24
    2.3   CIP Identification 26
    2.4   CIP Approval...27
    2.5   CIP Execution 29
    2.6   CIP Assessment..31
    2.7   CIP Closing...33
    2.8   University CIP Team Members' Perception
            about Factors Related to CIP Success 33
    2.9   Conclusions 34

PART II   Successful CIPs

Chapter 3   Reduction of Ambulance Response Time 37

     3.1   CIP Resume 37
     3.2   CIP Description 38
     3.3   Factors Related to CIP Success 49
     3.4   References 52

Chapter 4   Increasing the Fulfillment Level in a Wire and
Cable Company 55

     4.1   CIP Resume 55
     4.2   CIP Description 56
     4.3   Factors Related to CIP Success 65
     4.4   References 68

Chapter 5   Setup Time Reduction in a Packaging Line in the
Beverage Industry 69

     5.1   CIP Resume 69
     5.2   CIP Description 70
     5.3   Factors Related to CIP Success 80
     5.4   References 83

Chapter 6   Material Waste Reduction in the Food Industry 85

     6.1   CIP Resume 85
     6.2   CIP Description 86
     6.3   Factors Related to CIP Success 98
     6.4   References 101

Chapter 7   Critical Success Factors for Continuous
Improvement Projects: A Multi Case Study 103

     7.1   Introduction 103
     7.2   Research Method 103
     7.3   Results 105
     7.4   Summary..112
     7.5   References 113

PART III Less Successful and Unsuccessful CIPs

Chapter 8 Less Successful CIPs 117

    8.1   Introduction 117

    8.2   Less Successful CIPs: Reduction of a Production
          Line Stop Causes by Storage 119

    8.3   Less Successful CIPs: Reduction of Sale
          Opportunity in an International Hardware
          Organization 122

    8.4   Conclusions 125

    8.5   References 126

Chapter 9 Unsuccessful CIPs 127

    9.1   Introduction 127

    9.2   Unsuccessful CIP: Inventory Management in a
          Small Size Manufacturing Organization 128

    9.3   Unsuccessful CIP: Transportation Cost
          Reduction in an Automotive Manufacturing
          Organization 130

    9.4   Conclusions 133

    9.5   References 133

Summary

Chapter 10 Summary 135

    10.1   Introduction 135

    10.2   Summary Part I – Continuous Improvement
          Projects Overview 135

    10.3   Summary Part II – Successful CIPs 136

    10.4   Summary Part III – Less Successful and
          Unsuccessful CIPs 138

    10.5   Critical Success Factors for CIPs 138

    10.6   Limitations 141

    10.7   Future Work 141

Index 143

Preface

During our professional and academic life we had the opportunity to lead, facilitate, co-advise, or be a team member on more than 30 CIPs. We have been witnesses to incredible improvements and the excitement of team members, customers, and stakeholders from a successful CIP. Unfortunately, we have also seen the frustration, agony, desperation, and the loss of time that produce an unsuccessful CIP. Some authors state that manufacturing and services organizations are having problems achieving initial CIP goals and sustaining initial results. Also, researchers indicate that unsuccessful CIPs have an impact on the organization employees' motivation and the organization's continuous improvement initiative. For these reasons, we have been studying and conducting research about the factors related to CIPs success since 2015; learning from successful, less successful, and unsuccessful CIPs.

Therefore, we decided to integrate valuable information related to manning or leading CIPs, factors related to CIP success, and lack of factors that produce less successful CIPs, or unsuccessful CIPs in this book.

Acknowledgements

We would like to thank our institutions for the support received to produce this work. Also, we would like to thank our editorial team for assisting us with the publication of this book. Finally, we would like to express our deepest gratitude to our following colleagues who contributed to the enrichment of this work by sharing their knowledge and experiences of continuous improvement projects through the case studies included in chapters of this book:

Jesús Alexis Torrecillas, MBA,
Director of Industrial and Systems Engineering Academic Program, Universidad de Monterrey

Dr. Jesús Vázquez,
Independent Consultant and Professor, Department of Engineering, Universidad de Monterrey

Dr. Teresa Verduzco,
Associate Professor, Department of Engineering, Universidad de Monterrey

Dr. Bernardo Villarreal,
Professor, Department of Engineering, Universidad de Monterrey

Dr. Edgar Marco Aurelio Granda,
Director of Engineering and Technology Graduate

Programs, Universidad de Monterrey

Ana Veronica Rodriguez,
Ph.D. Student, Universidad de Monterrey

Andrea Montalvo,
Alumni, Industrial and Systems Engineering, Universidad de Monterrey

Samantha Lankenau,
Alumni, Industrial and Systems Engineering, Universidad de Monterrey

Ana Cristina Bastidas,
Alumni, Industrial and Systems Engineering, Universidad de Monterrey

Mitzary Elizabeth Chavero,
Alumni, Industrial and Systems Engineering, Universidad de Monterrey

Yaneth Alejandra Santos,
Alumni, Industrial and Systems Engineering, Universidad de Monterrey

Alan Javier Corral,
Alumni, Industrial and Systems Engineering, Universidad de Monterrey

Catalina Uriquidi,
Alumni, Industrial and Systems Engineering, Universidad de Monterrey

Melissa Lopez,
Alumni, Industrial and Systems Engineering, Universidad de Monterrey

Pedro Daniel Vazquez,
Alumni, Industrial and Systems Engineering, Universidad de Monterrey

Melissa Grace González,
Alumni, Industrial and Systems Engineering, Universidad de Monterrey

Mauricio Alejandro Garza,
Alumni, Industrial and Systems Engineering, Universidad de Monterrey

Saul Antonio Villa,
Alumni, Industrial and Systems Engineering, Universidad de Monterrey

About the Authors

 **Fernando González Aleu** has more than 15 years experience in higher education organizations as a part-time undergraduate professor and thesis advisor (10 years), Industrial and Systems Engineering Program Director (2 years), and currently as a full-time Associate Professor in the Department of Engineering (4 years). Currently, Fernando is teaching the following courses: Quality, Productivity, and Competitiveness (undergraduate level) General Systems Theory (undergraduate level), Senior Project (undergraduate level), and Research Seminar (graduate level). Prior industry experience includes 15 years implementing quality systems, environmental systems, and management systems in Mexico and Chile. Overall, academic and practitioner, Fernando has led/facilitated more than 30 continuous improvement projects and co-advised another 15.

Fernando received a BS in Mechanical and Management Engineering at Universidad de Monterrey (UDEM), an MS at Instituto Tecnológico y de Estudios Superiores de Monterrey (ITESM) in 1999, and both an MS and Ph.D. in Industrial and Systems Engineering from Virginia Tech in 2015 and 2016, respectively. His research is focused on continuous improvement projects and performance excellence models, producing one book chapter, four journal papers, and 22 conference proceedings. He is a member of the Institute of Industrial and Systems Engineers, the American Society for Engineering Management, the American Society for Quality, and the Industrial Engineering and Operations Management Society.

Some of the honorary and services positions developed by Fernando include Board of Director of the Quality and Patient Safety at Christus Health (2018 – present), Board of Director at Society for Engineering and Management Systems (2018 – present), and Research Candidate at Mexico's National Research System (2017 – present).

**Prof. Jose Arturo Garza-Reyes** is Professor of Operations Management and Head of the Centre for Supply Chain Improvement at the University of Derby, UK. He is actively involved in industrial projects where he combines his knowledge, expertise, and industrial experience in operations management to help organisations achieve excellence in their internal functions and supply chains. As a leading academic, he has led and managed international research projects funded by the European Commission, British Academy, British Council, and Mexico's National Council of Science and Technology (CONACYT). He has published extensively in leading scientific journals, including the *International Journal of Production Research*, *International Journal of Production Economics*, *Journal of Cleaner Production*, *Production Planning & Control*, *Supply Chain Management: An International Journal*, *TQM & Business Excellence*, *Journal of Manufacturing Technology Management*, etc., and a number of international conferences. Professor Garza-Reyes has also published four books in the areas of operations management and innovation, manufacturing performance measurement, and quality management systems. He is co-founder and current Editor of the *International Journal of Supply Chain and Operations Resilience* (Inderscience), Associate Editor of the *International Journal of Production and Operations Management*, Associate Editor of the *Journal of Manufacturing Technology Management*, and Editor-in-Chief of the *International Journal of Industrial Engineering and Operations Management*. Professor Garza-Reyes has also led and guest edited special issues *for Supply Chain Management: An International Journal*, *International Journal of Lean Six Sigma*, *International Journal of Lean Enterprise Research*, *International Journal of Engineering Management and Economics*, and *International Journal of Engineering and Technology Innovation*. Areas of expertise and interest for Professor Garza-Reyes include general aspects of operations and manufacturing management, business excellence, quality improvement, and performance measurement. He is a Chartered Engineer (CEng), a certified Six Sigma-Green Belt, and has over eight years of industrial experience working as Production Manager, Production Engineer, and Operations Manager for several international and local companies in both the UK and Mexico. He is also a fellow member of the Higher Education Academy (FHEA) and a member of the Institution of Engineering Technology (MIET).

Introduction

In a global market or in highly competitive conditions, organizations (manufacturing, service, or government) need to work in a concept called performance excellence or operational excellence, which is defined as "an integrated approach to organizational performance management that results in: (1) delivery of ever-improving value to customers, contributing to organizational sustainability; (2) improvement of overall organizational effectiveness and capabilities; and (3) organizational and personal learning" (Blazey, 2008, p. 333). Three well-known performance excellence (PE) models developed by private or government institutions are the Malcolm Baldrige National Quality Award (MBNQA), the European Foundation for Quality Management (EFQM) Excellence Model, and the Shingo Model. These three PE models share similar goals, which could be synthesized to increase and sustain operational excellence.

An important component of these PE models is the application of continuous improvement concepts or initiatives through the entire organization. For example, organizations applying for the MBNQA need to describe how their performance measurement systems identify projects of continuous improvement or innovation, as well as how these projects are conducted. Another focus for continuous improvement observed in the Shingo model (which has a guiding principle called scientific thinking) is the innovation and/or improvement obtained by repetitive cycles of observation, experimentation, and learning (e.g. plan-do-check-act or plan-do-study-act, Six Sigma, and Lean Six Sigma). Therefore, continuous improvement initiatives are highly important for organizations interested in improving and sustaining their process performance.

For those organizations that decide to base their continuous improvement efforts applying any type of improvement projects initiatives, such as Six Sigma, Lean Six Sigma, Lean, general quality improvement projects, quality circles, Kaizen events, and others, it is important that they master continuous improvement projects, including project identification, developing, closing, and sustainability. Although there is valuable information in the current literature about continuous improvement projects' (CIPs) hard outcomes and perceived outcomes as well as CIP success factors, to the authors' knowledge, these publications limited the authors in the number of words, impacting the quality of knowledge that the readers could obtain from journal papers or conference proceedings. Additionally, publications describing or investigating failure of CIPs are extremely limited.

Therefore, the purposes of this book are to offer a deep understanding of how to conduct CIPs, how to apply different CIP methodologies, and how to identify the success factors for CIPs. In order to achieve these goals, the authors structured this book in the following chapters: CIP overview, managing CIPs, successful CIPs, less successful CIPs, unsuccessful CIPs, and behaviors to achieve outstanding CIP results. CIP overview addresses topics such as the definition of a CIP, types of CIP, metrics to measure CIP success, and factors related to CIP success. Managing CIPs describes the conceptual framework used to identify, approve, execute, assess, and close a CIP. This framework was the same used in each case study included in the subsequent chapters. Successful CIPs consists of five case studies where the authors offer in-depth information about CIP execution and an analysis of the factors that impact on CIP success. The analysis of these factors includes a survey answered by most of the CIP team members. Less successful CIPs is a section where the authors also offer in-depth information about CIPs that suffered some major problems during the execution (e.g. CIP took more time, team members having to leave the CIP team, or the CIP goal was not achieved). To conduct the analysis of these CIPs, interviews and surveys were conducted with CIP leaders and some CIP team members. Unsuccessful CIPs is a chapter that includes a case study where the CIP was closed during the project timeframe. As in the previous chapter, interviews and surveys were conducted with the CIP leader. Lastly, behaviors to achieve outstanding CIP results compares the difference between factors and behaviors, proposing a list of behaviors that should be present during CIP execution in order to obtain exceptional and sustainable CIP results.

Part I

Continuous Improvement Projects and Success Factors

Improvement is part of our daily activities in different aspects of our lives, finding a better route to work, reducing time waiting in the traffic, increasing the productivity of a production line, and buying more with less. Since the beginning of the quality movement, continuous improvement projects have been crucial for organizations in order to improve their process and performance metrics. Part I is composed of three chapters which offer an overall view of continuous improvement projects (Chapter 1); the efforts of a university to disseminate and manage continuous improvement projects amongst their Industrial and Systems Engineering senior students (Chapter 2); and the results from an empirical study of success factors related to continuous improvement projects (Chapter 3).

1

Continuous Improvement Projects (CIPs) Overview

1.1 INTRODUCTION

Continuous improvement and innovation are essential elements to the competitiveness of modern organizations around the world, and a keystone in different performance excellence models, such as the Malcolm Baldridge National Quality Award (MBNAQ), the European Foundation for Quality Management (EFQM) Excellence Award, and the Shingo Prize. In order to address continuous improvement and/or innovation requirements, organizations could implement the following initiatives: quality circles, continuous improvement projects (CIPs), teamwork, a suggestions mailbox, and many others.

This book focuses on CIPs and, in this Chapter, we define and explain relevant concepts related to CIPs, types of CIPs most frequently used, characteristics of successful CIPs, and factors related to their success. This information is crucial to have a clearer understanding of the information presented in the case studies included in the subsequent chapters.

1.2 WHAT IS A CIP?

There are several tools or mechanisms under the umbrella of Kaizen, or continuous improvement; initiatives to help organizations improve their operational excellence, e.g. suggestion mailbox, total productivity maintenance, CIPs, and quality circles (Imai, 1986). CIPs are defined as dedicated team-based processes, typically with different backgrounds or from different departments, working to improve process performance metrics and systems with or without minimal capital investment in a relatively short time, such as a day or several months (González Aleu and

Van Aken, 2017; González-Aleu et al., 2018); for example, quality improvement projects (plan-do-check-act or plan-do-study-act), Lean Six Sigma projects, Kaizen events, and Six Sigma projects. From this definition, a CIP has the following key characteristics: team-based, cross-functional, minimal capital investment, relatively short timeframe.

1.3 TYPES OF CIPs

As it was mentioned in the previous section, there are several types of CIPs that have been used by different organizations. According to the literature (González Aleu and Van Aken, 2016), the application of CIPs has been increasing over the last two decades. The most common types of CIPs and their definitions are shown in Table 1.1. For the purpose of this book, a CIP (González Aleu, 2016):

- May use different improvement methodologies/tools and be known by different names. For example, a CIP may use Lean tools such as 5S or value stream mapping (and be called a Kaizen event, Lean project, rapid improvement event, or Lean event). It may use DMAIC (and be called a Six Sigma project). It may use a combined approach between Six Sigma and Lean (and be called a Lean Six Sigma project), or it may use a general improvement approach such as plan-do-check/study-act – PDCA or PDSA – (and be called a process improvement project or quality improvement project). In this book, these are all referred to as CIPs.
- May occur in a different timeframe. For instance, a CIP may take a day or few days from start to finish (such as with a Kaizen event or Lean event) or it may take several months (such as with a Lean Six Sigma project or Six Sigma project). CIP has a defined beginning vs. being a "standing" permanent team.
- May have one or more defined improvement goals focused on quality (such as errors or rework), costs, efficiency, timeliness, customer satisfaction, etc.
- May have minimal budget or investment to implement changes recommended or identified.

Although quality circles could be interpreted as CIPs, they have two important differences. First, in quality circles team members are the same over time (e.g. every time that production line "A" conducts a quality circle,

TABLE 1.1

Types of CIP and definitions

Type of CIP	Definition
General quality improvement project	Also known as process improvement project or just quality improvement project, is defined "as an organized effort on the part of three or more individuals with a designated team leader or facilitators to resolve a specific problem or undertaken activities to improve upon current practices that goes beyond the routine daily operation of the department or functional activity, or the normal responsibilities of a quality assurance committee" (Weiner, et al., 1997, p. 497)
Kaizen event	"A focused and structured improvement project, using a dedicated cross-functional team to improve a targeted area, with specific goals, in an accelerated timeframe" (Farris et al., 2008, p. 10)
Six Sigma project	The application of a rigorous problem solving methodology (define, measure, analyze, improve, and control – DMAIC) and advanced statistical tools (e.g. inference statistics, statistical process control and design of experiments) to reduce process variability (Breyfogle, 2003; Tang et al., 2007)
Lean Six Sigma project	Project focused on reducing process variability or eliminating waste through the integration of the rigorous Six Sigma project solving methodology (DMAIC) and advanced statistical tools, with Lean Production principals and tools.(Delgado et al., 2010; Furterer, 2016)

their team members will be the same), but in CIP teams are integrated for a specific project and dissolve when the project is finished. Second, quality circles use team members from the same target area and CIP used cross-functional team members, according to the CIP goal to achieve.

1.4 WHAT IS A SUCCESSFUL CIP?

CIPs, like any other type of project, have hard and soft metrics to assess the level of success. Hard metrics are quantitative performance metrics, such as the percentage of goal achievement, the percentage of target area impact, the percentage of CIP advanced/delayed, etc. For the purpose of this book, a successful CIP has two performance metrics: achieved or exceeded CIP main goal and finished in the timeframe proposed (most of the CIP documented in this book had a timespan of 16 weeks). Less

TABLE 1.2

CIP customer perceived impact

Survey items
This CIP improved the performance of the target area
Overall, this CIP helped people in the target area work together to improve performance
This CIP achieved its overall goals/objectives
Overall, this CIP was a success
This CIP has a positive effect on the target area
The target area improved measurable as a result of this CIP
Changes made to the target area as a result of the CIP are still in effect
Improvements in outcomes made to the target area as a result of the CIP have been sustained
Project stakeholders/customers believe this CIP was a success
The CIP met stakeholder/customer requirements and expectations
Project stakeholders/customers were satisfied with the results of this project
Overall, this CIP helped people in the target area work together to improve performance
This CIP achieved its overall goals/objectives

successful CIPs are those CIPs that failed to achieve one of these two performance metrics. If the CIP fails to achieve both performance metrics, then this CIP is considered unsuccessful.

There some CIPs where the initial main goal was defined very ambitiously (hard to achieve), affecting both metrics used to assess CIP success. On the other hand, there are also some situations where the CIP goal defined was very relaxed (easy to achieve), producing a lack of satisfaction of the customer (owner of the CIP) with the team performance. Therefore, it is important to use an assessment tool to measure customer satisfaction with the CIP. Table 1.2 shows thirteen survey items used to assess CIP customer perceived impact (González Aleu, 2016).

Once that the CIP was closed, the CIP customer could answer survey items from Table 1.2 using a six-point agreement scale (1 = strongly disagree to 6 = strongly agree).

1.5 FACTORS RELATED TO CIP SUCCESS

The most detailed list of factors related to CIP success was developed by González Aleu and Van Aken (2016) using a systematic literature review and these factors are classified into four categories. First, task design involves nine factors related to CIP goal definition, task area complexity, and task area commitment to continuous improvement initiatives. Second, team design involves nine factors related to the process used to select CIP team members and CIP team constitution characteristics. Third, the CIP process involves 10 factors related to the internal processes existing in a CIP team during the execution of a CIP. Fourth, organization involves 25 factors related to the organization profile, tangible and intangible organization resources assigned to CIPs, leadership, and continuous improvement program support. Factors from each category are defined and its importance to achieve CIP success is supported by one or two citations from different researchers or practitioners using quotes and citations (see Table 1.3 – Task design, Table 1.4 – Team design, Table 1.5 – CIP process, and Table 1.6 – Organization)

TABLE 1.3

Task design factors

Factor name	Definition	Quote	Citation
Goal development process	Development of goals by CIP team members during the project	"After analyzing water use throughout the plant during the previous year, the QIT came up with a goal of reducing water consumption by 15%"	Anonymous, 1996, p. 75
Goal clarity	Extent to which CIP goal(s) are clear to CIP team members and stakeholders	"The statement should present a specific and quantifiable goal so that the criteria for success are clearly understood and testable"	Tamm et al., 2012, p. 1532
Goal difficulty	Level of difficulty, technical challenge, or complexity of CIP goal(s)	"If limited efficiency savings targets of 2.5% or 3% are set, then people will aim to achieve just these. But there's no incentive to go way beyond this and seek, for example, savings of 25 to 30%"	Bagley and Lewis, 2008, p. 10
Goal alignment	Alignment of CIP goal(s) with organizational goals, objectives, strategies, and/or priorities	"Six sigma projects are linked directly to an organization's business metrics and bottom line"	Gijo, 2011, p. 27

(Continued)

TABLE 1.3 (*Continued*)

Task design factors

Factor name	Definition	Quote	Citation
Project duration	Time span (days, weeks, or months) for the completion of the CIP	"Because it's designed [Action Workout] to work in 60-day timeframes, we believed this system would allow us sufficient time to test, refine and expand as we deployed"	Bolton, 2004, p. 63
Problem scope	Size and nature of the problem addressed by the CIP, in terms of number of employees, physical space, organizational processes and functional boundaries, and breadth of problem areas targeted	"One of the foremost considerations in selecting a Green Belt project is whether it can be easily completed"	Ho et al., 2008, p. 266; Table 4
Target area routineness	Level of complexity of the target area, in terms of product mix, process stability, and employee turnover	"Another limitation of the study was the use of one specific work environment: modular homebuilding. Although modular homebuilding is essentially a residential construction processes, this industry has characteristics of manufacturing attributed to standardized processes and controlled environments".	Ikuma et al., 2010, p. 559
Target area commitment to change	Commitment of target area employees to change	"Change can only succeed if the people who do the work feel that the improvement is better than what they were doing before the change, and they have the confidence to carry it out"	West, 2012, p. 52
Target area understanding of continuous improvement	Understanding by target area employees of continuous improvement principles, methodologies, and tools used by the CIP team	"Even though project shows fruitful results, it faced typical hurdles in its path such as lack of knowledge about the methodology, lack of resources, non-availability of data"	Bhat et al., 2014, p. 637

TABLE 1.4

Team design factors

Factor name	Definition	Quote	Citation
Team member experience	Experience of team members (including leader) with previous CIPs	"What this adds up to is an environment in which some people attend a certification program merely to gain the certification, not to gain a thorough understanding of Six Sigma. As a result, we end up with 'certified' BBs without any hands-on experience, making project completion in the real work almost impossible"	Gijo, 2011 p. 28
Team autonomy	Level of control that team members have over CIP activities and decisions	"The researchers learned that the workers overall were very willing to make improvements, especially when they could be in control of those changes"	Ikuma et al., 2010, p. 559
Stakeholder representation	Representation from key stakeholders (e.g., customer, suppliers, production employees, supervisors, etc.) on CIP team	"The participation of Operators of the processes, Operations Management, Process Engineers, Health, Safety, Environmental and Security Department, Design Engineers and support of management was critical to the success of these projects"	Jacoby, 2009, p. 45
Cross-functionality	Representation from a breadth of functional roles and expertise (e.g., quality, engineering, purchasing, scheduling, IT, HR, etc.) on CIP team	"The team for our body MR imaging project consisted of radiologists with experience in body MR imaging, a senior nurse, a technologist supervisor with extensive experience as an MR imaging technologist, an MR imaging administrator, a systems analyst, and a facilitator with a background in process improvement engineering"	Tamm et al., 2012, p. 1532

(Continued)

TABLE 1.4 (*Continued*)

Team design factors

Factor name	Definition	Quote	Citation
Target area representation	Representation of target area employees on CIP team	"Pitfall: You don't have the right people on the improvement team. Recommendation: The team should represent staff members who are affected by the problem. Keep the number of team participant small – no more than six to eight people who can represent their peers".	West, 2012, p. 50
Internal team roles	Use of clear team roles and responsibilities on CIP team	"Develop a set of action steps, decide on the sequence and assign responsibility for each step to a team member"	Schultz, 2011, p. 38
External champion/ sponsor	Support, guidance, and approval provided by champion(s)/sponsor(s) external to CIP team	"Achieving process improvement with financial impact requires that projects be strategically selected by the company, owned by a Champion and led by a specially trained project leader"	Ward et al., 2008, p. 50
Team size	Number of people directly participating as members of CIP team	"Pitfall: You don't have the right people on the improvement team. Recommendations: The team should represent staff members who are affected by the problem. Keep the number of team participant small – no more than six to eight people who can represent their peers".	West, 2012, p. 50
Team improvement skills	Team members' knowledge and skills in problem-solving, improvement, and change management methodologies and tools	"There is a hierarchy in a Six Sigma project and each individual has a specific level of knowledge and skills that should enable that individual to accomplish designated tasks"	Alarifi and Alamri, 2014, p. 19.

TABLE 1.5

CIP process factors

Factor name	Definition	Quote	Citation
Team commitment to change	CIP team members' commitment and accountability to improve the target area and to achieve CIP goals	"Critical success factor: Team involvement and commitment"	Tlapa et al., 2014, p. 820; Table 1
Team harmony	Environment and culture within the team	"Project success also depends on selecting the right goals, the right team and the right atmosphere for the project."	Gijo, 2011, p. 29
Team communication and coordination	Activities performed by CIP to communicate, interact, and coordinate efforts within the team	"I meet regularly with my Green Belt project group"	Ho et al., 2008, p. 267; Table 4
Action orientation	Extent to which CIP team has a focus on action including data collection, experimentation/testing, and implementation	"Our team spent as much time as possible in the work area"	Farris et al., 2009, p. 60; Table A1
Tool appropriateness	Appropriateness of problem-solving and improvement tools used to analyze and solve problems	"By applying such design of experiment, we were able to achieve the objective of determining the most influence inputs which have significant effect on chipping size, identifying the appropriate conditions for each significant input to achieve good dice line quality"	Jamaluddin, 2011, p. 34
Structured methodology	Extent to which improvement methodology is systematic, well-defined, and executed thoroughly	"We have successfully implemented our improvement plans based on Six Sigma's DMAIC methodology. As a result, we can reduce CTQ (Y1) from 803,030 DPMO to 139 DPMO"	Kim et al., 2010, p. 644

(Continued)

TABLE 1.5 *(Continued)*

CIP process factors

Factor name	Definition	Quote	Citation
Solution iterations	Use of multiple solution iterations by CIP team to explore and test alternative solutions	"The time-table of the workshop is shown in Table 2. It was shaped so that enough time was ensured for realizing concepts and ideas into practice by repeating changeover activity and improving it bit by bit with every trial"	Štefanić, 2010, p. 64
Planning for institutionalization	Planning activities conducted by CIP for development of new work procedures, delivery of training on new work procedures, creation of new performance measures related to new processes, etc.	"It is very important for Kaizen process to be successful to make all good moves and changes (tried during the workshop) standard working procedure so that it could become base for next Kaizen steps"	Štefanić, 2010, p. 64
CIP progress reporting	Extent to which CIP team reports on progress to higher-level management and other stakeholders (e.g., peers in the target area) throughout the project	"Driving forces: good working relations, clear objectives, timely client feedback, client support and commitment, regular meetings/reviews, and help and concern"	Voehl, 2004, p. 362
CIP technical documentation	Documentation and dissemination of information to stakeholders on goal achievement, changes made to processes (new procedures), data and findings, other outcomes, and recommendations	"Once the CIP [community improvement project] is finalized, the policies and procedures must be documented"	Voehl, 2004, p. 357

TABLE 1.6

Organization factors

Factor name	Definition	Quote	Citation
General management support	Support of higher-level managers for the CIP and its goals	"The participation of Operators of the processes, Operations Management, Process Engineers, Health, Safety, Environmental and Security Department, Design Engineers and support of management was critical to the success of these projects"	Jacoby, 2009, p. 45
Management involvement	Participation of higher-level managers in activities to support CIP during launch, throughout project (e.g., progress meetings), and during report out	"For instance, Six Sigma is a very distinct approach. Six Sigma is an analytical method that employs finely tuned statistical tools, where management and steering committees are involved and considerable funds have to be allocated"	Demers, 2002, p. 33
Management understanding of continuous improvement	Higher-level managers' understanding of improvement principles, methodologies, and tools used by CIP team	"Ensure understanding of the kaizen method and purpose throughout the work crew and management"	Ikuma, 2010, p. 559
CIP planning	Activities conducted before CIP launch to plan and coordinate the CIP (e.g., team member selection, goal definition, arranging resources, data and document gathering, etc.)	"The written team charter should specifically outline the charge of the team, its goals and objectives"	Sifner, 2012, p. 8
Project identification and selection	Activities conducted to identify and select a CIP out of possible candidates	"Project selection [from the section of Four Factors Critical to Success]. Each project supports the following criteria: provides a direct link to the strategic goals of the organization, directly impacts key business objectives, improves a process in a measurable way, financial contribution, and direct benefits to key customers"	Ward et al., 2008, p. 51

(Continued)

TABLE 1.6 (*Continued*)

Organization factors

Factor name	Definition	Quote	Citation
CIP priority	Relative priority of a CIP as compared to other CIPs and other major initiatives	"We also included a variable called Major, with 3 for high-priority projects, 2 for medium-priority projects, and 1 for low-priority projects"	Choo, 2014, p. 1468
Information from previous CIPs	Availability of information from previous relevant CIPs	"If I encounter problems with my Green Belt project, I can seek explanations from the knowledge management system database"	Ho et al., 2008, p. 267; Table 4
Financial resources	Availability of financial resources (money) to CIPs needed to complete the project	"Driving forces: necessary financial resources and financial control capability"	Voehl, 2004, p. 362
Team member time	Ability of CIP members to allocate necessary time needed for the project	"All of the participants had important day jobs, but they had to put their regular jobs on-hold while they committed 100% of their effort to one or more lean events"	Askins et al., 2011, p. 4
General resource support	Availability of general resources needed to support the project	"Even though project shows fruitful results, it faced typical hurdles in its path such as lack of knowledge about the methodology, lack of resources, non-availability of data"	Bhat et al., 2014, p. 637
Materials and equipment	Availability of materials and equipment needed to support the project	"This one-and-a-half-day training session ensured universal discipline for using the unique team improvement process in a box provided as part of Action Workout. It is literally a kit with everything the team needs to complete its assignment, including guidebooks, posters, worksheets, sticky notes and pens. The kit helped us conduct short, 90-minute weekly team meetings"	Bolton, 2004, p. 64

(*Continued*)

TABLE 1.6 (*Continued*)

Organization factors

Factor name	Definition	Quote	Citation
Software	Availability of software (e.g., for statistical analysis, project management, process mapping, etc.) to CIP needed to support the project	"I use Excel and statistical analysis software to analyze project data"	Ho et al., 2008, p. 267; Table 4
Facilitation	Facilitation, guidance, and coaching available to improvement project team throughout the project	"Then early on it was decided that the Quality Council would act more like a coordinating body than a controlling body, and if teams needed any help they were free to consult with the Quality Council for ideas on ways to move forward"	Fairfield-Sonn, 1999, p. 58
Data availability	Access for CIP to data needed for the project	"Even though project shows fruitful results, it faced typical hurdles in its path such as lack of knowledge about the methodology, lack of resources, non-availability of data"	Bhat et al., 2014, p. 637
Data trustworthiness	Credibility and reliability of data used by CIP team	"I am concerned about the AMQIP data reliability and validity"	Gandhi, 2000, p. 116; Table 3
Training	Availability of training needed for CIP team members to conduct the CIP	"Past proposals for improvement have been poorly handled because of muddled implementation, lack of resources, inadequate training or the eventual abandonment of activities, only to have remedies replaced by another program of the month"	Schultz, 2011, p. 35
Recognition and rewards	Incentives, recognition, and rewards provided to team members for achievement of CIP goals	"The organization decided to provide coaching, counselling and training to the people involved in the project; giving rewards and sharing profits of the project with its employees to motivate them	Kumar et al., 2007, p. 863

(*Continued*)

TABLE 1.6 *(Continued)*

Organization factors

Factor name	Definition	Quote	Citation
		to bring about a cultural change within the organization; recognizing and reinforcing desired improvement alternatives and desired behaviors, which includes a periodic project review between management and the people responsible for improvement activities"	
Performance evaluation/review	Impact of achievement of CIP goals on performance evaluation/review for employees serving on CIP team	"Lean/Six Sigma project targets must be incorporated into reintegrated Black Belts and all employees (including management) performance contracts"	Mashinini-Dlamini and van Waveren, 2013, p. 1995
Organizational policies and procedures	Alignment of organizational policies/procedures with CIP activities and goals	"Another challenge we faced in conducting a Lean project at KATH was addressing the need for change in the context of Ghanaian cultural norms and traditional health care roles"	Carter et al., 2012, p. 341
Organizational culture	Alignment of values and beliefs of the surrounding organization with CIP activities and goals	"Another challenge we faced in conducting a Lean project at KATH was addressing the need for change in the context of Ghanaian cultural norms and traditional health care roles"	Carter et al., 2012, p. 341
Organizational structure	Alignment of organizational roles, responsibilities, and structure with CIP activities and goals	"Six Sigma is unique in terms of its roles, responsibilities, and team work that are built on the business process model of the organizational structure"	Alarifi and Alamri, 2014, p. 19

(Continued)

TABLE 1.6 (*Continued*)

Organization factors

Factor name	Definition	Quote	Citation
Support from continuous improvement program	Support to the CIP from a structured continuous improvement program (e.g., continuous improvement program coordinator, standard training materials, standard improvement process, etc.)	"Residents with an institutional QI process are more likely to have initiated a QI project"	Choudhery et al., 2014, p. 855
Follow-up activities	Follow-up activities after CIP is completed to ensure changes are continued, action items are completed, and results are sustained	"Often the most neglected or deferred action of the PAT is the follow-up"	Sifner, 2012, p. 9
Lessons learned	Documentation of lessons learned from the CIP experience with respect to the team itself and how it worked	"The three agenda items should be: What went well? 'What didn't work?' Asking for the positive first helps team members realize how much they were able to accomplish"	West, 2012, p. 52
Deployment of changes	Extent to which changes made by CIP team are deployed to other relevant processes outside the team's scope	"After this, the Lean Six Sigma strategy has been transferred to other facilities in the same group, outside of Sweden, with similar results"	Andersson et al., 2014, p. 919

Several researchers have been studying these factors in manufacturing or services organization using retrospective studies (e.g. CIP leader/facilitators answered a survey based on his/her experience in a CIP finished one month or more ago). Three main findings could be found:

- The top 10 factors more frequently mentioned in the literature are structured methodology, tool appropriateness, stakeholder representation, data availability, target area commitment to change, general management support, management involvement, cross-functionality, CIP progress reporting, and project identification and selection (González Aleu and Van Aken, 2016). From a category perspective, one out of nine task design factors (11%), two out of nine team design factors (22%), three out of 10 CIP process factors (30%), and four out of 25 organization factors (16%) were included in the list of top 10 factors. This information suggests that CIP process factors have a predominant impact on CIP success.

- The top 10 factors more important (scale 1 = not at all important to 6 = extremely important) to achieve CIP success, from 116 CIP leader/facilitators in hospitals, were goal clarity (5.38), goal alignment (5.30), target area representation (5.27), target area commitment to change (5.24), general management support (5.23), data trustworthiness (5.22), stakeholder representation (5.20), team commitment to change (5.17), goal development process (5.15), and data availability (5.08). From category perspective, four out of nine task design factors (44%), two out of nine team design factors (22%), one out of 10 CIP process factors (10%), and three out of 25 organization factors (12%) were included in the list of top 10 factors (González-Aleu et al., 2018). This information suggests that task design factors have a predominant impact on CIP success.

- Sixteen out of the 53 factors shows statistically a significant difference in the level of importance depending on the type of CIP conducted (González-Aleu et al., 2018).

As it is observed from the evidence collected from other investigations, is not clear which factors could be the most important or with the highest impact on CIP success. Also, papers and proceedings mentioning the importance of some factors to achieve a successful CIP did not conduct a formal investigation on this matter; their comments are based on CIP team perceptions documented in the discussion section of the paper. This situation makes it difficult for CIP leaders/facilitators, and/or CIP team members to have a clear idea about which factors could be considered crucial in the achievement of a successful CIP. Therefore, it is important to collect information from ongoing CIPs to increase the body of knowledge about CIPs and help practitioners to achieve successful CIPs.

1.6 CONCLUSIONS

Kaizen event, Lean Six Sigma projects, Six Sigma projects, and general quality improvement projects are the most common types of CIPs conducted in manufacturing and services organizations. An extensive systematic literature review (González Aleu and Van Aken, 2016) showed a list of 53 factors related to CIP success. These factors have been studied in different time using different metrics such as the frequency of mention in the literature and the level of importance to achieve CIP success from retrospective surveys (CIP leader/facilitator answered a survey based in a CIP finished more than one year ago). These metrics indicate a lack of agreement about the most important factors related to CIP success. In order to increase the knowledge about CIPs and how to obtain better results from them, a Mexican university has been conducting CIPs and documenting case studies using information from CIP team members.

During the following chapter, we will describe how this Mexican university manages these CIPs, collect information from CIP team members, and document case studies.

1.7 REFERENCES

Alarifi, S. A., & Alamri, A. (2014). HPT and six sigma: Is there a difference that matters? *Performance Improvement*, 53(7), 14–22.

Andersson, R., Hilletofth, P., Manfredsson, P., & Hilmola, O. P. (2014). Lean six sigma strategy in telecom manufacturing. *Industrial Management & Data Systems*, 114(6), 904–921.

Anonymous (1996). Continuous improvement process. *Dairy Foods*, 97(13), 75.

Askins, B. R., Davis, S. R., Heitzman, K. S., & Olsen, R. A. (2011). The Application of Lean Thinking Principles and Kaizen Practices for the Successful Development and Implementation of the Ares IX Flight Test Rocket and Mission.

Bagley, A., & Lewis, E. (2008). Debate: Why aren't we all lean? *Public Money & Management,* 28(1), 10–11.

Bhat, S., Gijo, E. V., & Jnanesh, N. A. (2014). Application of lean six sigma methodology in the registration process of a hospital. *International Journal of Productivity and Performance Management,* 63(5), 613–643.

Bolton, M. (2004). Get staff involved in quality initiatives. *Quality Progress,* 37(2), 62.

Breyfogle, F. W., III (2003). *Implementing Six Sigma: Smarter Solutions Using Statistical Methods.* Hoboken, NJ: John Wiley & Sons.

Carter, P. M., Desmond, J. S., Akanbobnaab, C., Oteng, R. A., Rominski, S. D., Barsan, W. G., & Cunningham, R. M. (2012). Optimizing clinical operations as part of a global emergency medicine initiative in Kumasi, Ghana: Application of lean manufacturing principals to low-resource health systems. *Academic Emergency Medicine,* 19(3), 338–347.

Choo, A. S. (2014). Defining problems fast and slow: The u-shaped effect of problem definition time on project duration. *Production and Operations Management,* 23(8), 1462–1479.

Choudhery, S., Richter, M., Anene, A., Xi, Y., Browning, T., Chason, D., & Morriss, M. C. (2014). Practice quality improvement during residency: Where do we stand and where can we improve? *Academic Radiology,* 21(7), 851–858.

Delgado, C., Ferreira, M., & Castelo Branco, M. (2010). The implementation of lean six sigma in financial services organizations. *Journal of Manufacturing Technology Management,* 21(4), 512–523.

Demers, J. (2002). The lean philosophy. *CMA Magazine,* 76(7), 31–33.

Fairfield-Sonn, J. W. (1999). Influence of context on process improvement teams: Leadership from a distance. *The Journal of Business and Economic Studies,* 5(2), 47–66.

Farris, J. A., Van Aken, E. M., Doolen, T. L., & Worley, J. (2008). Learning from less successful Kaizen events: A case study. *Engineering Management Journal,* 20(3), 10–20.

Farris, J. A., Van Aken, E. M., Doolen, T. L., & Worley, J. (2009). Critical success factors for human resource outcomes in Kaizen events: An empirical study. *International Journal of Production Economics,* 117(1), 42–65.

Furterer, S. L. (2016). *Lean Six Sigma in Service: Applications and Case Studies.* Boca Raton, FL: CRC Press.

Gandhi, T. K., Puopolo, A. L., Dasse, P., Haas, J. S., Burstin, H. R., Cook, E. F., & Brennan, T. A. (2000). Obstacles to collaborative quality improvement: The case of ambulatory general medical care. *International Journal for Quality in Health Care,* 12(2), 115–123.

Gijo, E. V. (2011). 11 ways to sink your six sigma project. *Lean & Six Sigma Review,* 11(1), 27.

González Aleu, F., & Van Aken, E. M. (2016). Systematic literature review of critical success factors for continuous improvement projects. *International Journal of Lean Six Sigma,* 7(3), 214–232.

González Aleu, F., & Van Aken, E. M. (2017). Continuous improvement projects: An authorship bibliometric analysis. *International Journal of Health Care Quality Assurance,* 30(5), 467–476.

González Aleu, G. F. (2016). *An Empirical Investigation of Critical Success Factors for Continuous Improvement Projects in Hospitals.* Doctoral dissertation, Virginia Tech.

González-Aleu, F., Van Aken, E. M., Cross, J., & Glover, W. J. (2018). Continuous improvement project within Kaizen: Critical success factors in hospitals. *The TQM Journal*, 30(4), 335–355.

Ho, Y. C., Chang, O. C., & Wang, W. B. (2008). An empirical study of key success factors for six sigma green belt projects at an Asian MRO company. *Journal of Air Transport Management*, 14(5), 263–269.

Ikuma, L. H., Nahmens, I., & James, J. (2010). Use of safety and lean integrated kaizen to improve performance in modular homebuilding. *Journal of Construction Engineering and Management*, 137(7), 551–560.

Imai, M. (1986). *Kaizen*. New York: Random House Business Division.

Jacoby, J. (2009). *Pollution Prevention through the Application of Six Sigma and Lean.* Doctoral dissertation, Saint Louis University.

Jamaluddin, Z., Razali, A. M., & Mustafa, Z. (2011, September) Wafer dice process improvement using six sigma approach. In *2011 IEEE International Conference on Quality and Reliability* (pp. 31–35). IEEE.

Kim, Y., Jeong Kim, E., & Gyo Chung, M. (2010). A six sigma-based method to renovate information services: Focusing on information acquisition process. *Library Hi Tech*, 28(4), 632–647.

Kumar, M., Antony, J., Antony, F. J., & Madu, C. N. (2007). Winning customer loyalty in an automotive company through six sigma: A case study. *Quality and Reliability Engineering International*, 23(7), 849–866.

Mashinini-Dlamini, N. F., & van Waveren, C. C. (2013, July) Exploring critical success factors for the reintegration of lean six sigma black belts into line function roles in the technology environment. In *2013 Proceedings of PICMET'13: Technology Management in the IT-Driven Services (PICMET)* (pp. 1990–1997). IEEE.

Schultz, J. R. (2011). Pushback prevention. *Quality Progress*, 44(8), 32.

Sifner, T. A. (2012). Process action team in health care. *Performance Improvement*, 51(5), 7–11.

Štefanić, N., Tošanović, N., & Čala, I. (2010). Applying the lean system in the process industry. *Strojarstvo*, 52(1), 59–67.

Tamm, E. P., Szklaruk, J., Puthooran, L., Stone, D., Stevens, B. L., & Modaro, C. (2012). Quality initiatives: Planning, setting up, and carrying out radiology process improvement projects. *Radiographics*, 32(5), 1529–1542.

Tang, L. C., Goh, T. N., Yam, H. S., & Yoap, T. (2007). *Six Sigma: Advanced Tools for Black Belts and Master Black Belts*. West Sussex, UK: John Wiley & Sons.

Tlapa, D., Limon, J., Baez, Y., & Valles-Rosales, D. J. (2014, December). Critical success factors of six sigma: An overview. In *2014 IEEE International Conference on Industrial Engineering and Engineering Management* (pp. 818–822). IEEE.

Voehl, F. (2004). Six sigma community improvement projects. In *ASQ World Conference on Quality and Improvement Proceedings* (Vol. 58, p. 351). American Society for Quality.

Ward, S. W., Poling, S. R., & Clipp, P. (2008). Selecting successful six sigma projects: successful six sigma projects are the result of careful selection, planning and execution. *Quality*, 47(10), 50–52.

Weiner, B. J., Shortell, S. M., & Alexander, J. (1997). Promoting clinical involvement in hospital quality improvement efforts: the effects of top management, board, and physician leadership. *Health Services Research*, 32(4), 491.

West, B. (2012). Rapid cycle improvement: Avoid the pitfalls. *Nursing Management*, 43(11), 50–53.

2

Managing CIPs

2.1 INTRODUCTION

As we mentioned in the previous chapter, continuous improvement projects (CIPs) are important to those organizations interested in being competitive and/or implementing a performance excellence model. There are different types of CIPs (e.g. Kaizen event, Lean Six Sigma project, Six Sigma project, and general quality improvement project, etc.), and there is a lack of agreement about the level of importance of the 53 factors related to CIP success, see Chapter 1. After having analyzed a significant number of journal papers and conference proceedings, we believe that the documentation of ongoing CIPs, through a case study format, will help practitioners to obtain a deeper understanding about CIPs and how they can be deployed in an efficient way.

Considering that most types of CIPs have an average duration greater than three months (only a Kaizen event has an average duration of less than a week), the data collection process from ongoing CIPs will take several months. Therefore, we decided to use information from senior projects conducted by Industrial and Systems Engineering (ISE) undergraduate students from a Mexican university as the source of CIPs. We define a senior project, or capstone project, as a CIP conducted by three or four students during 16 weeks (or more) to solve an specific and defined problem in a manufacturing or service organization using methodologies such as DMAIC (Define, Measure, Analyze, Improve, and Control), PDCA (Plan, Do, Check, and Act), General System Intervention Process, or others. The senior projects are a requirement for each ISE undergraduate senior student (in his/her last semester) in order to obtain a bachelor's degree.

During this chapter, we will offer extended information regarding the evolution of the senior projects at the Mexican university, how senior projects are managed, and ISE undergraduate students' perception about the factors related to CIP (senior project) success.

2.2 SENIOR PROJECT INEXHAUSTIBLE SOURCE OF CIPs

Government institutions, manufacturing organizations, and service organizations have the opportunity to use senior undergraduate students to conduct CIPs for free, or with a relatively low cost.

Since 1982, Industrial and Systems Engineering (ISE) senior students at a Mexican university have undertaken a senior project as the last task that every student has to address in order to receive a bachelor's degree. This senior project process has been transformed over time (see Figure 2.1), presenting the following improvements:

- The beginning (1982–1985): every senior project was developed individually (no teams). Main topics addressed were quality, production, planning and control, and time and motion studies.
- Growing (1986–1991): if the students wished and the senior project scope allowed it, students could conduct their senior projects in a team of two (50% of the senior projects were conducted as part of a team). The predominant topics were quality, systems engineering, economic analysis (for investments), and production optimization.
- Stabilization (1992–1996): a new director for the ISE program arrived and he was responsible for creating a procedure from the senior project approval to the senior project close. The percentage of senior projects conducted in a team reduced slightly to 49%. The predominant topics were quality, systems engineering, optimization, logistics, and planning and control.
- Internationalization (1997–2000): students requested to conduct their senior projects in the U.S. The senior project system or process was updated to give students the opportunity to perform their senior projects outside Mexico. Also, in 1998 a student used the Six Sigma methodology for the first time (the result of a senior

project conducted in a General Electric plant in Mexico) and a faculty member presented a senior project in the 1999 ISERC (now IISE) Annual Conference and Expo. The percentage of senior projects conducted as a team continued dropping to 29%. The predominant topics were the same as in the previous period of time.

- Continuous improvement projects (2001 – currently): five major changes were observed in the senior project process. First, topics such as 5S's, Six Sigma, Lean, and logistics predominated in the local industries, forcing the students to solve organizational problems using these tools and methodologies. Second, as a result from a previous course, where the students had to create an imaginary consulting firm (including name, vision, mission, roles, etc.), students developed different skills such as oral communication skills and application of structured methodologies such as DMAIC, PDCA (or PDSA), and general processes of system intervention. Third, senior projects had to be conducted as part of a team in with between two and three members. Special cases where students decided to conduct a senior project without a team or where the team was composed of four students were analyzed by the senior project committee. During this period, 94% of the senior projects were conducted as a team, whereas only 1.3% of these were developed based on four team members. Fourth, new faculties began to send their students projects to compete for Best Paper Student Competitions (IEOM Annual Conference and IISE Annual Conference); winning on several occasions. Fifth, in 2017 the university began isolated efforts to measure factors related to senior project projects or CIP success. Between 2000 and 2017, a total of 462 senior projects have been conducted under the modality of CIP. From now on, the senior project will be referred to as a CIP.
- Research project (2015 – currently): this is overlapping with the previous period of time. As the number of students conducting a double degree (bachelor's degree at Mexican university and master's degree with U.S. universities or European universities) and the number of CIP faculties with a Ph.D. increased, ISE programs offered these students the option of conducting individual research projects using the systematic literature review approach.

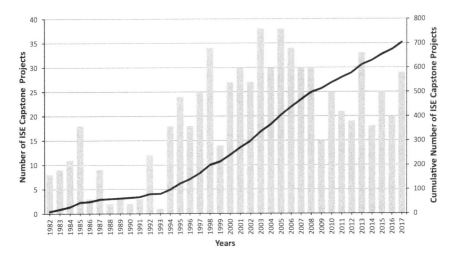

FIGURE 2.1
Frequency of ISE senior projects at Mexican university

From 2001 to 2017, an average of 27 CIPs per year were conducted by the ISE students at the Mexican institution. These CIPs and the current CIPs have been managed using five stages (CIP identification, CIP approval, CIP execution, CIP assessment, and CIP closing), with six main actors: ISE program directors (equivalent to continuous improvement program manager), internal and external faculties (equivalent to CIP leader/facilitator), students (university CIP team members), faculty evaluator (these are usually CIP leader/facilitator from other CIPs), customer organization (responsible of the target area where the CIP will be conducted), and organization stakeholder employees (organization CIP team members). Each of these stages is documented in the following sections.

2.3 CIP IDENTIFICATION

The continuous improvement (CI) program manager has an initial meeting with the university CIP team members (only ISE students) to share key information such as proposal deadline, proposal presentation, documentation to fill during the different stages of the CIP.University CIP team members are responsible for finding their own CIP in a local or international organization (in this case, students and/or the organization have to pay for the travel expenses). To perform this activity, university CIP team members use personal contacts, faculty contacts or cold contacts. Once that an organization is interested in conducting a CIP, the university CIP team members meet with the customer organization, identify organization CIP team members, document a proposal using the format requested by the CI program manager, and submit their proposal to the CIP committee (CIP leaders; only internal faculties). University CIP team members are allowed to submit only one proposal.

2.4 CIP APPROVAL

The CI program manager schedules a meeting with the CIP committee (only internal faculties) to hear university CIP team members' presentations (10 minutes). During these presentations, the CIP committee assesses each proposal using the following criteria: CIP title, CIP problem or need description, CIP main goal and secondary goals, CIP conceptual framework, CIP methodology, CIP scope, CIP timeframe, references, and CIP organization contributions. Each criteria is assessed (see Figure 2.2) using a five-point scale (1 = deficient, 2 = poor, 3 = acceptable, 4 = good, and 5 = outstanding). After the proposal presentation is concluded, CIP committee members have five minutes for a question and answer session. Then, university CIP team members leave the room and the CIP committee deliberates the CIP proposal result.

There are three different CIP proposal results: accepted as it is, accepted with changes, and rejected. University CIP team members with a rejected CIP proposal should decide if they improve their CIP proposal or find a new CIP in a new organization or the same company. If the university CIP team members decide to find a new CIP in a new organization, they have to formally close the relationship with the current organization sending a letter describing the situation and thanking them for the time and opportunity offered.

University CIP team members with a rejected CIP proposal during the first presentation have the opportunity to present the new CIP proposal using the same procedure described earlier. If the CIP proposal is not accepted this time, the university CIP team members should close the relationship with the organization and they will have to wait until the next semester to submit a new CIP proposal.

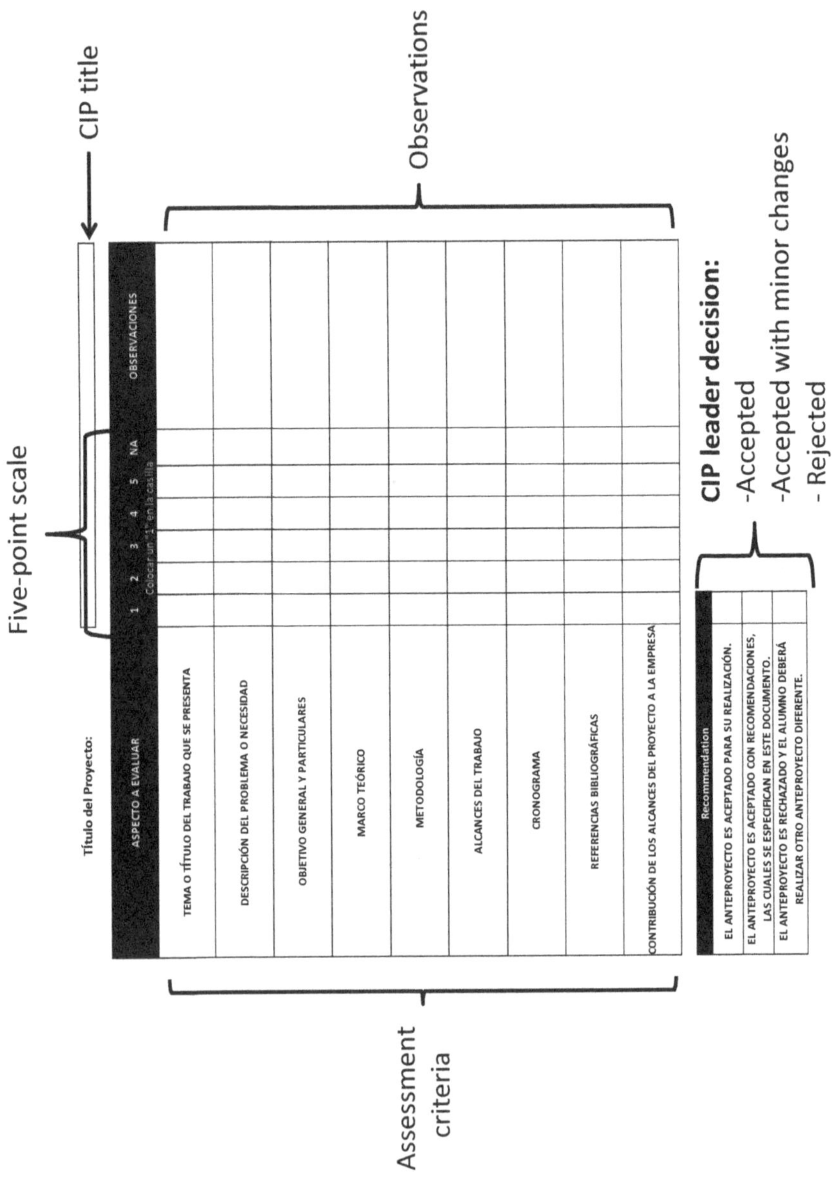

FIGURE 2.2
CIP proposal assessment

With the CIP proposals accepted, the CI program manager and the CIP committee decide which faculty will be assigned as CIP leader/facilitator; as well as which faculties will be assigned as an evaluator. The responsibility of a faculty evaluator is to assess the university CIP team member's performance three times during the CIP timeframe (see section on CIP assessment). The CIP leader/facilitator and faculty evaluator are assigned based on topic preference and the possibility of publishing the CIP project in conference proceedings or a journal.

2.5 CIP EXECUTION

Unless the university CIP team members request more time at the beginning of their CIP, every CIP should be completed in 16 weeks (the equivalent of an academic semester at the Mexican university). The CIP execution is more easily understood using the diagram in Figure 2.3. Each university CIP team member has to work a minimum of 25 hours per week on the CIP (inside or outside the organization) following each step of the methodology used to solve the problem (e.g. DMAIC or PDCA). They are responsible for collecting data from front line operations, coordinate

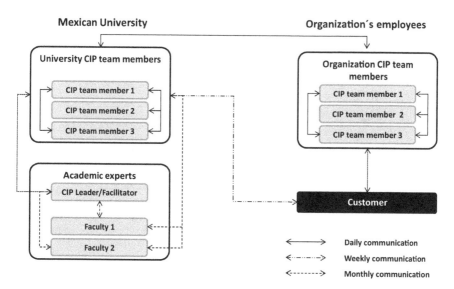

FIGURE 2.3
CIP execution

cause–effect analysis, implement solutions, validate results, and coordinate meetings with CIP leader and faculties. For that reason, they have to be in contact with the organization CIP team members, which participate in the CIP in addition to their day-to-day activities. Organization CIP team members have the role to provide historical data, participate in the cause-effect analysis, and implement solutions.

Every week, during the 16 weeks of the CIP timeframe, the CIP leader meets with the university CIP team members for about an hour. During this meeting, the CIP leader reviews which activities the university CIP team members spent their time on and how much time. In this way, CIP leaders validate that each university CIP team member worked 25 hours or more in the CIP (see Figure 2.4). Otherwise, the CIP leader records a lack of time spent on the project. Also, during these weekly meetings, the CIP leader solves doubts from university CIP team members, which include the type of methodology to use, how to apply a tool, type of additional analysis to conduct, etc. Sometimes, when the CIP leader does not have the solution from the university CIP team members' questions, he/

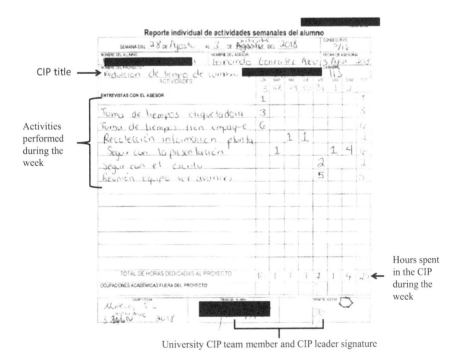

FIGURE 2.4
Individual record of university CIP team-member activities

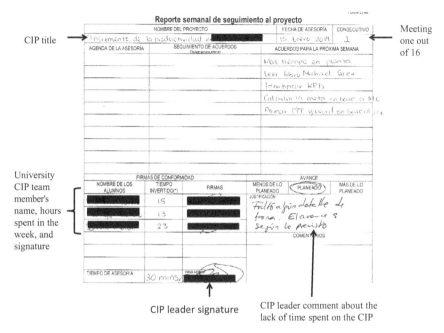

FIGURE 2.5
CIP team weekly meeting record

she may request to have an additional meeting with one or two of the faculties. Records from these weekly meetings include the following information (see Figure 2.5): agenda, follow up on activities from the previous week, new activities to complete by the following meeting, CIP progress status (late, on time, advance), justification of the CIP progress status, time spent by each university CIP team member in the week in the CIP, time spent by the CIP leader in the meeting (or other activities related to this CIP).

If required, the CIP leader is able to visit the organization (three times during the CIP timeframe), with the university CIP team members, to increase his/her knowledge about the place where they will be working.

2.6 CIP ASSESSMENT

There are two progress meetings where university CIP team members show evidence of the CIP progress status. The first progress meeting is conducted during week five of the academic semester and the faculties expect to have evidence of a clear understanding of the project, CIP goals clearly defined, cause–effect analysis finished, and a list of potential solutions. The second progress meeting is conducted during week ten, where university CIP team members have to show evidence that all solutions were implemented. During these meetings, the CIP leader keeps a record of the conversations (questions and answers) between university CIP team members and both faculties (see Figure 2.6). At the end, both faculties assign a grade (from 0 to 100) to each university CIP team member (grade could be the same as the rest of the group or different for each member) and reported to the CI program manager.

As we know, there are some CIPs showing a CIP progress status of late during the first or second meeting. This situation could be originated by several factors, such as lack of support from the organization, university CIP team members' lack of time spent on the CIP, university CIP team members lack the knowledge to solve the problem, etc. In this situation, faculties and CIP leaders have to decide if the CIP is too far away from the timeframe and assigned the status of conditioned to next meeting results, or cancel the CIP. Any of these statuses should be reported to the CI program manager.

FIGURE 2.6
Progress meeting assessment

2.7 CIP CLOSING

Two meetings are carried out to close the CIP in the following order: closing meeting at the university and a closing meeting with the customer. During the closing meeting at the university, the mechanism used to assess CIP progress are the same as mentioned in above. With the difference that CIP under the status of conditioned projects are not allowed to have a closing meeting. After this meeting, the university CIP team members with a grade of 70 or higher are called ISE engineers and can attend to the graduation and commencement ceremonies. However, they still need to conduct a final meeting with the customer. This meeting is the last one and the university CIP team members have to integrate faculties' and CIP leader's comments from the closing meeting.

2.8 UNIVERSITY CIP TEAM MEMBERS' PERCEPTION ABOUT FACTORS RELATED TO CIP SUCCESS

For the first time, university CIP team members whose CIP proposals were approved in Spring 2019 completed, during the first week of their CIP, a survey about the level of importance (1 = not at all important to 6 = extremely important) of each of the 53 factors (see Chapter 1) related to CIP success on achieving a successful CIP. Table 2.1 shows the descriptive statistics of the top 10 most important factors obtained from this study. Considering that university CIP team members do not have previous expertise in participating in a CIP, they consider CIP progress category as the most important; 6 out of 10 factors from this category are included in the top 10. On the other hand, it is also interesting to observe that there is not a single factor related to task design in the top 10 list; goal clarity was ranked in 13th place (mean = 5.44 and SD = 1.12).

TABLE 2.1

University CIP team members' perception about factors related to CIP success

Category	Factors Name	Mean	Std. Deviation
CIP progress	Team commitment to change	5.85	0.46
CIP progress	Planning for institutionalization	5.59	0.50
CIP progress	CIP technical documentation	5.59	1.05

(Continued)

TABLE 2.1 *(Continued)*

University CIP team members' perception about factors related to CIP success

Category	Factors Name	Mean	Std. Deviation
Organization	Lessons learned	5.56	0.64
CIP progress	Tool appropriateness	5.56	0.64
CIP progress	Team harmony	5.52	0.70
Organization	General management support	5.48	0.80
CIP progress	Structured methodology	5.48	0.80
Organization	Team member time	5.48	0.89
Team design	Team improvement skills	5.44	0.51

2.9 CONCLUSIONS

Throughout this chapter, we offered detailed information about senior projects as a source for CIPs, how university CIPs are managed, and university CIP team members' perception about factors related to CIP success. Considering that university CIP team members have no previous experience participating in CIPs, the difference between Table 2.1 and the information presented in Chapter 1 does not come as a surprise.

During the elaboration of this book, the authors are not aware of any journal or conference paper that analyzes the 53 factors related to CIP success from ongoing CIPs. Therefore, five ongoing CIPs were documented as case studies in this book, from the CIP identification to CIP closing stages. These case studies will be valuable information for CIP leaders/facilitators, academics responsible to manage other senior projects, and researchers interested in investigating factors related to CIP success.

Part II

Successful CIPs

The purposes of these chapters are three: to understand how different successful CIPs were managed, learn about the application of problem-solving methodologies or tools from CIPs, and identify the factors related to CIP success. To achieve these aims, the authors included four chapters describing CIP implementations from three different industry sectors: health service (case A), basic metal production (case B), and drink and food (case C and case D). An additional chapter was included at the end of this part to identify the critical success factors related to CIP success.

Each case study was structured in three sections. First, the CIP resume includes aspects about CIP background and CIP management such as CIP team members, CIP goal, type of CIP used, CIP performance metrics (percentage of goal achievement and percentage of target area improvement), CIP duration (weeks), and resources used during the CIP (such as CIP leader/facilitator time, and university CIP team members' time). Second, depending on the type of CIP used, a description of the activities and tools used in each step of the CIP (e.g. DMAIC or PDCA) were included to understand the flow that the CIP had. Third, when the CIP was closed, CIP team members (from university and organization) answered a survey about the importance of the 53 factors related to CIP success. Descriptive statistics about this survey are included in this section.

After these four case studies (Chapters 3, 4, 5, and 6), the authors conduct brief research from eight different CIPs and document their findings using the research journal article format, but easy to read for a practitioner, in Chapter 7. This chapter shows a list of the top ten factors highly related to CIP success.

3

Reduction of Ambulance Response Time

3.1 CIP RESUME

Emergency Medical Service (EMS) systems have the goal to provide urgent medical care to a patient in an emergency situation (such as pre-hospital care or emergency patient transportation to the nearest hospital). Several studies have been conducted to improve EMS systems performance (Bandara et al., 2014; Capar et al., 2017; Mashoufi et al., 2019) with a major focus on reducing response time (i.e. the time between the receipt of a call at the dispatch center and the arrival of the first emergency response vehicle at the scene) by placing the ambulances in optimal locations (Blackwell et al., 2009; Burke et al., 2013; Pons et al., 2005; Sultan et al., 2019; Yu & Huang, 2017). However, performance metrics such as the average ambulance hour utilization (i.e. the number of services divided by the ambulance hours used) and the ambulance turnaround time (i.e. time from ambulance hospital arrival until it is available to respond to another emergency) should be analyzed to improve EMS performance operations.

A major supplier of EMS in the Monterrey metropolitan area, which includes seven counties from the state of Nuevo Leon with more than 2 million inhabitants, has 34 ambulances to offer its services on a continuous basis of 24 hours/day during 365 days/year. In 2015, this company provided its EMS services on more than 35,400 occasions. The lack of current resources (i.e. ambulance vehicles and financial) to satisfy EMS demand required the elimination or reduction of waste during different steps of the ambulance turnaround time. Therefore, the purpose of this CIP was to increase the number of ambulance services in the Monterrey metropolitan area with a response time of less than 10 minutes by 10%. The CIP team used General Process of System Interventions as the problem-solving methodology. This methodology consists of four steps: pre-diagnostic, analysis, design, and implementation. A variety of soft system tools and lean tools were used during the four stages of the problem-solving methodology. These included System Mapping, Overall Vehicle Effectiveness (OVE), Transportation Value Stream Mapping (TVSM), and Total Operational Vehicle Effectiveness (TOVE) to achieve CIP goals. At the end of this project, the CIP team increased the number of ambulance services in the Monterrey metropolitan area with a response time of less than 10 minutes by 36%.

This CIP was carried out during a 20 week period, from summer to fall 2016 by 6 CIP team members (i.e. one CIP leader/facilitator, three university CIP team members, and two organization CIP team members). The team spent a total of 1,920 hours in the CIP as follows: CIP leader/facilitator 20 hours and the university CIP team members 1,900 (31.6 hours per week per member). The time spent on the project by the organization CIP team members was not recorded.

3.2 CIP DESCRIPTION

This section presents the four stages, i.e. pre-diagnostic, analysis, design, and implementation, which the CIP went through when following the General Process of System Interventions problem-solving methodology.

3.2.1 Phase I: Pre-diagnostic

The pre-diagnostic phase has the aim to obtain a complete overview of the system or systems that will be intervened. Therefore, the university CIP team members conducted a literature review about EMS organizations and several interviews with CIP customers and stakeholders. The following paragraphs describe the main outcomes obtained from this phase.

The performance metrics of an EMS institution should be focused on measuring the agility to execute the delivery of the service in order to improve their performance and increase the possibility of saving more human lives. Some of the main EMS institution performance metrics are paramedic response time, ambulance turnaround time, ambulance cycle time, and patient stabilizing time at place or scene, among others. From these measures, the paramedic response time has become one of the main performance metrics used among EMS institutions to define a benchmark measure of the quality of the service provided (Pons et al., 2005); suggesting a target response time of ≤ 8 minutes for at least 90% of emergency responses. Also, for a successful cardiac and cerebral resuscitation, the International Guidelines 2000 Conference on Cardiopulmonary Resuscitation and Emergency Cardiovascular Care recommended a response time of 8 to 10 minutes (Blackwell et al., 2009). On the other hand, ambulance turnaround time is defined as the time that an ambulance takes to get ready to attend a new emergency; and it is calculated from the time when the ambulance vehicle arrives at a hospital until the time the same ambulance is available again to respond to new emergency calls (Burke et al., 2013). Furthermore, ambulance cycle time represents the total time taken by the ambulance from responding to an emergency call until it becomes available to respond to a new emergency call. Therefore, lower ambulance cycle times imply higher unit hour utilization and ambulance capacity; impacting the level of the organization's operating cost. Finally, a standard established for patient stabilizing time is a time of less than or equal to ten minutes; also called the Platinum Ten (Watson, 2001).

The EMS institution under investigation was established in 1937 and it is part of a large international organization with three main characteristics: service location, service lines, and EMS capacities. First, the EMS institution offered its services in Nuevo Leon, one of the 32 states that comprise Mexico, with a total of 5.12 million inhabitants. However, most of the services attended were focused in seven counties, also called Monterrey metropolitan area, with more than 2 million inhabitants. Second, there were five different lines of services offered by the EMS institution, i.e. EMS, medical services, youth and volunteers, ladies volunteers, and training. The CIP focused only on the EMS service. Third, there were 34 ambulances to offer their services 24 hours/day and during 365 days/year. Nevertheless, only 17 ambulances were available to operate. These 17 ambulances were assigned to 10 mobile bases and 7 to a fixed base.

A normal day operation of the EMS institution was observed to understand the different processes they undertook (see Figure 3.1). The Communications Center (CCOM) was the department of the EMS institution that received emergency reports and defined the need to send an ambulance after having identified that it really was a medical emergency. This department was made up of telephone operators, those in charge

of communication and image, and radio operators. Telephone operators were in charge of receiving the calls, capturing the service data in
the CCOM system and defining the need to send an ambulance. Once
the service was open, the radio operator was in charge of assigning an
ambulance to the patient to be later dispatched with two paramedics. In a
regular shift, there were three telephone operators and one radio operator.
When an ambulance was out of service, the paramedics assigned to that
unit were reassigned to the CCOM department to receive the calls. During
this observation process, a situation that captured the CIP team member's
attention was the limited access to historical data and the lack of global
positioning systems (GPS) an ambulance.

The CIP team members captured the information from more than
9,701 emergency services that the ESM institution responded to from
January to June 2016 in an Excel spreadsheet, identifying seven different steps (see Table 3.1). As mentioned earlier, paramedic response
time was a significantly important metric, where best EMS benchmark
institutions reported less than 10 minutes. However, the case EMS institution reported an average paramedic response time of 19.35 minutes,
which included the elapsed time from when the central office received
the emergency call and until the ambulance arrived at the place of the
emergency.

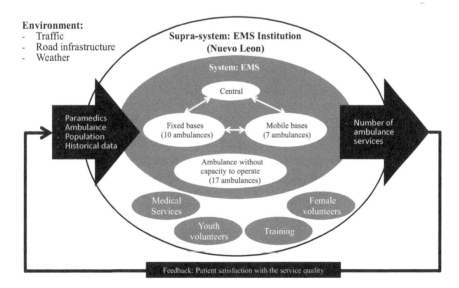

FIGURE 3.1
Emergency medical service mapping

TABLE 3.1

Steps of the emergency service

Steps	Definition	Mean (minutes)	SD (minutes)
Assignment	Elapsed time from the central office receives an emergency call to when the ambulance was assigned	5.00	7.90
Departure	Elapsed time from the when ambulance was assigned to the ambulance's departure from the base (fixed or mobile)	1.52	3.23
Arriving	Elapsed time from the ambulance departure from the base (fixed or mobile) to the ambulance arriving to the emergency place	12.83	9.48
Stabilization	Elapsed time from the ambulance arrival at the emergency place to when the patient is ready to be transported to hospital	14.78	12.08
Transportation	Elapsed time during the transportation of the patient to the hospital	23.02	65.48
Releasing	Elapsed time from the ambulance's arrival to the hospital emergency department to the ambulance's release from the hospital emergency department	49.52	108.87
Returning	Elapsed time from the ambulance's release by the hospital emergency department to the ambulance return to its base (fixed or mobile)	10.95	16.67

During a meeting with CIP customers and stakeholders, the CIP team defined the CIP goal as to increase the number of ambulance services in the Monterrey metropolitan area with a response time of less than 10 minutes by 10%. In order to achieve this goal, the ambulance response time had to be reduced (assignment time + departure time + arrival time). Several analyses were conducted to identify opportunities for improvement in the emergency service steps presented in Table 3.1.

3.2.2 Phase II: Analyze

Using the information captured in the Excel spreadsheet, which included contact, location, diagnostic, service code, date, hour, Guide Roji

(Monterrey metropolitan map), and others, four analyses were conducted. First, at least 81% of the emergency services showed one or more of the four categories of delays:

1) Distance (42.19%). An ambulance attended an emergency call outside its county;
2) Traffic (34%). An ambulance attended an emergency call in the following hours: 7:00–10:00, 12:00–13:00, and 16:00–19:00;
3) Assignment time (35.95%). The assignation of an ambulance took more than four minutes;
4) Departure time (18.47%). Ambulance departure from the base (fixed or mobile) took more than two minutes.

Second, Table 3.2 shows that the most common types of emergencies were sickness (40%), vehicle accident (31%), and accident (22%). On the other hand, considering the emergency call with a paramedic response time higher than 10 minutes, it was observed that the priority of the type of emergencies changed as follows: sickness (24.2 minutes), transportation (23.9 minutes), accident (22.4 minutes).

Third, a flow chart was created to map paramedic response time activities, identifying activities conducted by three main role players during a paramedic response time steps (i.e. call to assign, assign to departure, and departure to arrive): telephone operator, radio operator, and paramedic. Table 3.3 shows 13 activities in total. From these, 7 activities were classified as non-value added; consuming an average of 2.72 minutes (SD of 2.23 minutes)

TABLE 3.2

Emergency calls with a paramedic response time higher than 10 minutes

Type of emergency	Assignment (average time in minutes)	Departure (average time in minutes)	Arriving (average time in minutes)	Total (average time in minutes)
Sickness	6.10	1.88	16.22	24.2
Transportation (accidents other than vehicle)	6.15	1.4	16.35	23.9
Accident in house	5.35	1.88	15.17	22.4
Violence (e.g. shotgun and knife)	4.4	1.43	14.95	20.78
Vehicle accident	5.48	1.50	13.72	20.7

TABLE 3.3

Classification of paramedic response time activities

Paramedic response time steps	Activities	Actor	Equipment	Is this a value add activity?
Assignment	Receive an emergency call	Customer (not always is a patient)	Telephone	Yes
	Record the information of the service requested	Telephone operator	CCOM	Yes
	Observe if there is a new service open	Radio operator	CCOM	No
	Locate the nearest ambulance	Radio operator	Fleet management software	No
	Communicate to the ambulance the characteristics of the service requested	Radio operator	Fleet management software Radio	No
	Confirm that ambulance is informed about the service to perform	Paramedic	Fleet management software Radio	No
	Assign the ambulance to the patient or service	Radio operator	CCOM	Yes
Departure	Prepare to departure	Paramedic	N/A	No
	Communicate that ambulance is en route	Paramedic	Fleet management software Radio	No
	Update status of ambulance as "en route"	Radio operator	CCOM	Yes
Arriving	Transport to emergency location	Paramedic	N/A	No
	Communicate that ambulance arrive	Paramedic	Fleet management software Radio	Yes
	Update status of ambulance as "arrived"	Radio operator	CCOM	Yes

during the assignment and an average of 1.18 minutes (SD of 1.27 minutes) during the departure. Although transport to the emergency location was a non-value activity (arriving step) that consumed an average time of 12.83 minutes (SD of 9.48 minutes), this activity was highly related to factors outside CIP team control, e.g. traffic. Therefore, the CIP team member decided to exclude this activity from the CIP implementation.

Fourth, according to the data collected from ambulance services from January 1 to June 30 in 2016, ambulance utilization was analyzed during the three shifts, finding that 98.36% of the 17 ambulances available were used at least in one occasion during the three shifts (or day). However, considering that ambulance time was defined from the moment that one ambulance was assigned to service to the moment that it was free and ready for a new service, an average ambulance time per shift of 41 minutes was observed. This analysis showed that ambulances were attending the services for only 26% of the day and the remaining time they were not. After conducting several hypothesis tests using a p-value of 0.05, the CIP team identified that there was a statistically significant difference in the number of services attended between a different day of the week and between different shifts.

With this information in hand, the CIP team conducted a working session to generate a brainstorm (see Table 3.4) and create a tree current reality (see Figure 3.2), identifying the following root causes: the communication system between ambulance and the central office was deficient, there was not a defined procedure to assign the ambulance vehicle, and activities conducted by the central office were not well split. With these three root causes, the CIP team proposed some possible solutions as indicated in the following improvement phases.

TABLE 3.4

Brainstorm

No	Ideas
1	Semi-fixed point were defined in 1997 without an analysis
2	Demand analysis is done using paper maps
3	The coordinates from emergency services are not captured in a system to geolocated the ambulance
4	Semi-fixed ambulances do not change
5	According to the current demand, the assignation of bases (fixed and mobile) is not the best.

(Continued)

TABLE 3.4 (*Continued*)

Brainstorm

No	Ideas
6	Every time that there is an emergency service, the address of the service has to be written to send this information to the ambulance GPS
7	Radio operator does not able to visualize when a new emergency service was opened
8	Communication between telephonist and radio operator is deficient to open an emergency service
9	There is no interface between CCOM and Teletrac systems
10	The information systems available do not cover all the EMS organization needs
11	There is not a document procedure to assign the ambulances
12	Radio operators have a poor knowledge of the system used to assign ambulances
13	Radio operators use his/her instinct to assign an ambulance to an emergency service
14	In 37% of the emergency services ambulances have to cross counties to provide the service
15	Radio operators cancel emergency services at least once per shift because of a lack of ambulance availability
16	Ambulances have no communication system between GPS and radio operator
17	Ambulance status change is not exact
18	Visualization of ambulances available in real time is not exact
19	There is only one radio operator per shift
20	The three telephonists have a radio operator profile but are not used as radio operators
21	Ambulance departure takes a mean of 1:45 (minutes) with an SD of 3:30 (minutes)
22	Paramedics in a fixed base do not immediately see that a service has been assigned
23	Lack of coverage in the communication equipment (radio)
24	Notification of emergency service to paramedics is not standardized
25	Communication systems between CCOM and ambulances is poor
26	The capture of data related to the emergency service location is deficient
27	The cross streets are not double checked in Google maps beforehand to capture the information in the system
28	There are ambulances without GPS
29	The GPS currently available does not have a visualization screen to offer guidance to the paramedics
30	The current GPS does not visualize the exact point where the emergency service is needed
31	Paramedics have problems locating the exact point where the emergency service is needed
32	Waze (a GPS system) is available in the CCOM, but is not used

(*Continued*)

TABLE 3.4 (*Continued*)

Brainstorm

No	Ideas
33	Paramedics do not receive feedback about the best route to follow
34	Paramedics always decide the route to follow using their intuition and expertise
35	Paramedics never use the shortest route
36	Ambulances encounter traffic during the emergency service
37	There is a lack of route technology tools
38	Radio operators do activities that are not related to assigning ambulances
39	Communication systems when an emergency service is opened are verbal and not standardized
40	Radio operators capture the change of ambulance status manually
41	Radio operators takes 5:00 minutes with a standard deviation of 7:54 minutes to assign an ambulance to an emergency service
42	An ambulance takes more than 10 minutes to respond an emergency service
43	Message content between CCOM and ambulance is not standardized
44	There is not a system to assign the ambulance in shift
45	Activities and roles from the CCOM are not well distributed
46	Radio operators do administrative activities that are not their responsibility
47	Radio operators give support to the ambulance (paramedics) instead of only notifying them.
48	The analytic system to define improvement strategies could be better
49	Paramedics use paper maps to identify the location of the emergency service

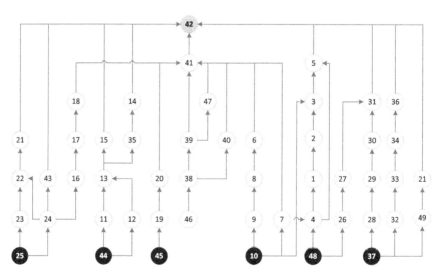

FIGURE 3.2
Tree current reality

3.2.3 Phase III: Design and Implementation

According to the analysis presented in the previous subsection, the CIP team worked in six potential solutions. The first solution consisted of reducing or eliminating the radio operator's non-value-added activities. Radio operators have a crucial role in the process of assigning an ambulance, performing eleven different activities, but there were only five value-added activities. From the six non-value-added activities, the CIP team considered that two should be performed by the radio operators (i.e. elaborate assistance reports and configuring shifts in the system), whereas the other four activities were suggested to be reassigned to other two departments or areas. These other four activities related to recording gasoline consumption (OMEGA), responding to ambulance failure reports (OMEGA), communicating the number of services attended (communication), and responding to resolutions from county (communication). The second solution consisted of training radio operators in the use of the navigation systems available in the company in order to locate the nearest ambulance to the emergency call. In order to implement the first and second improvement actions, the CIP team elaborated position descriptions, which were not available, and communicated these position descriptions to all the actors in the EMS organization. These actions were implemented during 10 of 16 of the CIPs. The third solution included the addition of a radio operator in the morning and afternoon, when most of the accidents happened. Although this action represented an extra cost for the EMS organization, the CIP team conducted a benchmarking with other public service organizations such as police and firefighters, identifying that some of these organizations used multiple radio operators. During week 11 out of the 16, the EMS organization hired a new radio operator and the CIP team trained the new employee using the position description elaborated. At this point, as it is observed, the first three improvement actions were related to the ambulance assignment. Other improvement actions were conducted to impact the performance metrics in the emergency service step.

The fourth solution focused on code visual aids. From the departure of the ambulance, paramedics need to be in constant communication with the radio operator (CCOM) mentioning the status of the service. There were different codes available to synthesize the status of a service such as 18 (understand), 10 (on my way), and 7 (arriving at the place of the emergency call). However, paramedics did not know all these codes, impacting also on the time spent by the radio operator to interpret paramedic information and including it in the system. Therefore the CIP team created a

FIGURE 3.3
Code visual aids

visual aid (see Figure 3.3) that included the seven most frequent codes used by a paramedic and a brochure with all the codes. These improvement actions were implemented in the 17 ambulances during the week 11 of the CIP and represented a minimum investment.

Paramedics used personal experience and book maps to identify the best route to drive in the city. Thus, as a fifth solution the CIP team suggested the acquisition of GPSs for each ambulance. An additional advantage that the integration of GPS to the ambulance had was that the radio operator could send the exact coordinates of the emergency call. A pilot test was conducted in two ambulances from weeks 8 to 13 of the CIP. Paramedics and radio operators identified initial problems in the transmission of the messages (i.e. two minutes' delay in message reception) because of poor installation of the antenna. After fixing this situation, message reception took 30 seconds and the ambulance arriving time was improved considerably. Unfortunately, the implementation of this improvement action required an investment of $6,460 US for 17 ambulances. Consequently, the EMS organization was not able to invest in this equipment.

The sixth solution consisted in the relocation of the ambulances. After analyzing the historical information of the emergency services per day of the week and hour of the day, the CIP team created a mathematical model to identify the best place for the relocation of the ambulances, in order that 76% of the emergency services could achieve the goal of arriving in 10 minutes or less. To implement a pilot test of these new locations, a group of paramedics visited the best places and defined the real location considering aspects such as parking areas and routes. These new locations were tested with 325 new services.

3.2.4 Phase IV: Results

After the design, implementation and monitoring of the actions mentioned in the previous sections, the CIP team achieved the improvement

TABLE 3.5

Ambulance response time improvement

Improvement actions	Ambulance response time per step	Before CIP	After CIP	Percentage of Improvement
1. Reduce radio operator non-value-added activities 2. Teach radio operator in the use of the navigation systems 3. Hire a second radio operator	Ambulance assign average time	5.00 minutes	4.08 minutes	18.4%
4. Code visual aids	Ambulance departure average time	1.52 minutes	1.05 minutes	30.9%
5. Utilization of GPS in ambulances 6. Relocation of ambulances	Ambulance arriving time	12.83 minutes	11.66 minutes	9.1%
	Ambulance response time	19.35 minutes	16.79 minutes	13.2%

of different performance metrics in the EMS organization (see Table 3.5). Overall, ambulance response time was reduced from 19.35 minutes to 16.79 minutes (13.2%)

The reduction of the time during the assignment, departure and arriving of the ambulance contributed to increasing the number of ambulances responding within 10 minutes, which represented an improvement from 16.4% to 36.6%. Therefore, the CIP goal was achieved.

3.3 FACTORS RELATED TO CIP SUCCESS

Considering that this CIP was finished on time, with a minimum investment, and achieving the initial goal, this CIP could be recognized as a successful CIP. From the information presented in this case study, there are several factors that could be related to CIP success, such as the use of advanced statistical tools, application of mathematical models, and the CIP team members' time (weekly hours) spent in the project. However, in order to increase the knowledge about the factors related to CIP success, a survey was applied at the end of the CIP to university CIP team members (see Table 3.6) using a six-point importance Likert scale (1 = not at all important, 2 = low importance, 3 = somewhat important, 4 = moderately important, 5 = very important, 6 = extremely important).

TABLE 3.6

Factors related to CIP success

	CIP team member 1	CIP team member 2	CIP team member 3	Mean	SD
Goal clarity	6	6	6	6.00	0.00
Target area representation	6	6	6	6.00	0.00
External champion/sponsor	6	6	6	6.00	0.00
General management support	6	6	6	6.00	0.00
Management involvement	6	6	6	6.00	0.00
Management understanding of CI	6	6	6	6.00	0.00
Team member time	6	6	6	6.00	0.00
Software	6	6	6	6.00	0.00
Facilitation	6	6	6	6.00	0.00
Data availability	6	6	6	6.00	0.00
Data trustworthiness	6	6	6	6.00	0.00
Team commitment to change	6	6	6	6.00	0.00
Team communication and coordination	6	6	6	6.00	0.00
Action orientation	6	6	6	6.00	0.00
Tool appropriateness	6	6	6	6.00	0.00
Structured methodology	6	6	6	6.00	0.00
Solution iterations	6	6	6	6.00	0.00
CIP progress reporting	6	6	6	6.00	0.00
CIP technical documentation	6	6	6	6.00	0.00
Goal alignment	6	6	5	5.67	0.47
Target area commitment to change	6	6	5	5.67	0.47
Stakeholder representation	5	6	6	5.67	0.47
Internal team roles	6	6	5	5.67	0.47
CIP priority	6	6	5	5.67	0.47
General resource support	5	6	6	5.67	0.47
Materials and equipment	5	6	6	5.67	0.47

(Continued)

TABLE 3.6 (*Continued*)

Factors related to CIP success

	CIP team member 1	CIP team member 2	CIP team member 3	Mean	SD
Organizational structure	6	6	5	5.67	0.47
Support from CI program	6	6	5	5.67	0.47
Team harmony	6	5	6	5.67	0.47
Planning for institutionalization	5	6	6	5.67	0.47
Target area understanding of CI	6	5	5	5.33	0.47
Team autonomy	6	5	5	5.33	0.47
Team improvement skills	5	6	5	5.33	0.47
Training	5	6	5	5.33	0.47
Organizational policies and procedures	5	6	5	5.33	0.47
Organizational culture	5	6	5	5.33	0.47
Follow-up activities	5	6	5	5.33	0.47
Lessons learned	5	6	5	5.33	0.47
CIP planning	6	6	4	5.33	0.94
Goal development process	5	5	5	5.00	0.00
Team size	5	5	4	4.67	0.47
Financial resources	4	5	4	4.33	0.47
Cross-functionality	5	5	3	4.33	0.94
Performance evaluation/review	5	5	3	4.33	0.94
Project identification and selection	4	3	6	4.33	1.25
Problem scope	5	6	2	4.33	1.70
Target area routineness	6	5	2	4.33	1.70
Goal difficulty	4	4	4	4.00	0.00
Information from previous CIPs	4	4	4	4.00	0.00
Team member experience	5	5	2	4.00	1.41
Project duration	4	3	4	3.67	0.47
Deployment of changes	4	4	3	3.67	0.47
Recognition and rewards	1	2	2	1.67	0.47

It is interesting to observe that 19 out of the 53 factors were considered by the three university CIP team members as extremely important (scoring 6 points) to achieve CIP success. Most of these 19 factors were focused in two categories: eight out of the 10 factors from the CIP process category (see Chapter 1, Table 1.5) and eight out of the 25 factors from organization category (see Chapter 1, Table 1.6). This evidence shows that the key for the success in this CIP was highly related to the way in which the CIP was conducted (i.e. tools, methodologies, pilot tests, and progress meetings and reports) as well as the support obtained from the organization, which included general manager support, data availability, and data trustworthiness.

Also, it is important to highlight that only three out of the 53 initial factors were considered by this CIP team as less than moderately important (i.e. project duration, deployment of changes, and recognition and rewards). This is interesting because this CIP team began its CIP four weeks early, then CIP team members did not suffer the pressure that other CIP teams usually have in terms of time constraint. Because this CIP involved all the emergency services offered by the EMS organization, then there was no need to deploy the improvement from this CIP to other sections in the organization. Finally, although the CIP success would lead to the CIP team members being awarded their bachelor's degree in Industrial Systems Engineering and the possibility of also obtaining a summa cum laude award; they did not consider these as relevant or motivational actors to achieve the CIP goal.

3.4 REFERENCES

Bandara, D., Mayorga, M. E., & McLay, L. A. (2014). Priority dispatching strategies for EMS systems. *Journal of the Operational Research Society*, 65(4), 572–587.

Blackwell, T. H., Kline, J. A., Willis, J. J., & Hicks, G. M. (2009). Lack of association between prehospital response times and patient outcomes. *Prehospital Emergency Care*, 13(4), 444–450.

Burke, L. G., Joyce, N., Baker, W. E., Biddinger, P. D., Dyer, K. S., Friedman, F. D., ... Sayah, A. (2013). The effect of an ambulance diversion ban on emergency department length of stay and ambulance turnaround time. *Annals of Emergency Medicine*, 61(3), 303–311.

Capar, I., Melouk, S. H., & Keskin, B. B. (2017). Alternative metrics to measure EMS system performance. *Journal of the Operational Research Society*, 68(7), 792–808.

Mashoufi, M., Ayatollahi, H., & Khorasani-Zavareh, D. (2019). Data quality assessment in emergency medical services: What are the stakeholders' perspectives? *Perspectives in Health Information Management*, 16(Winter), 1–20.

Pons, P. T., Haukoos, J. S., Bludworth, W., Cribley, T., Pons, K. A., & Markovchick, V. J. (2005). Paramedic response time: Does it affect patient survival? *Academic Emergency Medicine*, 12(7), 594–600.

Sultan, M., Abebe, Y., Tsadik, A. W., Ababa, A., Yesus, A. G., & Mould-Millman, N. K. (2019). Trends and barriers of emergency medical service use in Addis Ababa; Ethiopia. *BMC Emergency Medicine*, 19(1), 28.

Watson, L. (2001). The platinum ten. *Halstead: ResQMed*. Accessed January 8, 2018.

Yu, J. Y., & Huang, K. L. (2017, June). Improving emergency medical services with time-region-specific cruising ambulances. In *International Conference on Health Care Systems Engineering* (pp. 189–199). Springer, Cham.

4

Increasing the Fulfillment Level in a Wire and Cable Company

4.1 CIP RESUME

Order fulfillment involves aspects such as generating, filling, delivering, and servicing customer orders (Croxton, 2002). Order fulfillment is usually measured using three performance metrics, i.e. orders delivered on time, complete orders delivered, and product quality of delivered order. Although order fulfillment has been studied and documented from different perspectives, such as managing product variety in quotation processes (Cagliano, Kalchschmidt, Romano, & Salvador, 2005), IT-enhanced orders and delivery process of a fast-moving consumer goods (FMCG) company (Chung, Ching & Saad, 2007), and supplier selection and managing strategies, and manufacturing flexibility (Oly Ndubisi, 2005), it is interesting to observe that there are still companies having problems achieving satisfactory performance levels on order fulfillment.

An international company dedicated to manufacturing and supplying different types of wires and cables (e.g. energy cables, construction cables, magnetic wire, and electric cables) with more than 700 employees, had 51% of its orders delayed, affecting the fulfillment level of on-time orders by a monthly average of 88%. Considering that the highest fulfillment level achieved in 2015 was 98% and applying the entitlement approach (i.e. improve process performance by 70% in regards to the gap between the highest performance and average performance metric); the CIP team agreed with the customer to increase the fulfillment level by 7% (i.e. [98%–88%]*70%). In order to achieve this goal, the CIP team used the Deming's Plan-Do-Check-Act (PDCA) problem-solving methodology. After identifying the root causes and implementing five improvement actions (i.e. Kaizen events), in October 2016, the organization only failed to deliver on time, complete, and with the quality required by the customer in 1 out of every 40 orders, representing a fulfillment level of 97.5%, exceeding the CIP goal.

This CIP was developed over 16 weeks in the fall of 2016 by 5 CIP team members (one CIP leader/facilitator, three university CIP team members, and one organization CIP team-member) spending a total of 1,364 hours in the CIP as follow: CIP leader/facilitator 20 hours and the university CIP team members 1,344 (28 hours per week per member). The time spent on the project by the organization CIP team member was not recorded.

4.2 CIP DESCRIPTION

In order to identify the resources needed to conduct this CIP (i.e. people, financial, data), the CIP team created a detailed picture (Checkland & Scholes, 1999) of the process under study, see Figure 4.1. It consisted of nine steps: order reception, planning, production program, acquirements,

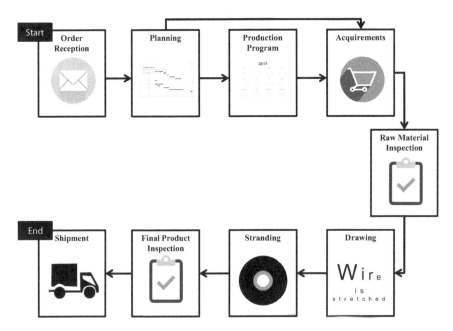

FIGURE 4.1
Rich picture of the process under study
(Adapted from Hidalgo-Chavero et al., 2017)

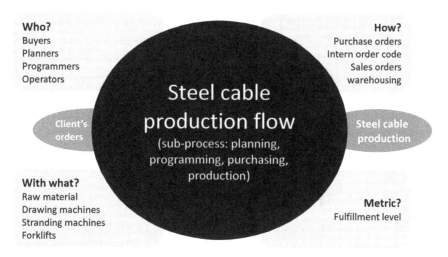

FIGURE 4.2
Turtle diagram of the entire process
(Adapted from Hidalgo-Chavero et al., 2017)

raw material inspection, drawing, stranding, final product inspection, and shipment. Additionally, a turtle diagram (Figure 4.2) was used to identify inputs, general processes, and outputs.

Both tools helped to identify four main resources for this CIP, namely: people, process knowledge, financial, and data. The CIP team was made up of three Industrial and Systems Engineering (ISE) senior students, one CIP facilitator, and one organization employee. The CIP team needed to increase its knowledge in regards to the production process and products of the wire and cable organization. Although a CIP does not require a major investment to implement improvement actions, a senior leader from the wire and cable organization defined a middle manager as responsible to approve any financial requirement from the potential improvement actions undertaken and deployed. The data was provided by the CIP organization employee and the ISE senior students evaluated data trustworthiness.

Once that the allocation of resources was determined, the CIP team then defined which problem-solving methodology to use. Based on the CIP team and the organization's previous knowledge, the intervention process was conducted following the Deming's Plan-Do-Check-Act (PDCA) problem-solving methodology. The first phase referred to the planning ('Plan') of the CIP. During this phase, it was necessary to establish the goals, define potential root causes, and propose potential solutions to overcome the problem addressed. After the "Plan" phase, the CIP embarked in the "Do" stage, which centered on testing the proposed solutions. On the other hand, the "Check" phase consisted of the analysis and verification of the results obtained from the "Do" stage of the project. If the results were not what the CIP team expected, then new solutions were sought. Finally, the "Act" phase referred to the implementation and standardization of the proposed solutions. Each of these four phases is described in more detail in the following sub-sections.

4.2.1 Phase I: Plan

A total of 526 orders taking in the full catalog of products including aluminum, copper and steel wired cables were placed in 2015. Steel wired cable orders represented 59% of the total amount of orders, or 46% of the total amount of tons produced. Therefore, the CIP team decided to narrow the scope of this CIP to only orders for steel products, which could be classified into three categories: stock, direct, and specials. First, stock orders represented 36% of steel production orders and these orders included products whose raw materials were already in the company's stock. Second, direct orders represented 58% of steel production orders and these included products that needed to take into account the supplier's lead-time. Third, special orders represented 6% of steel production orders and these included products whose raw materials required direct negotiation with the supplier.

In 2015, 142 orders of steel products failed to achieve fulfillment. These orders were initially considered by the CIP team to determine potential causes of failures. However, the lack of available and reliable data forced the CIP team to work with data from different databases in order to create a single Excel file to conduct an initial analysis. Unfortunately, 12 out of 142 orders were unable to be traced.

The remaining 130 orders were classified according to three types of failure, namely: waiting (produced on-time), quantity (amount of incorrect product), and quality (product with quality problems). As shown in the Venn diagram presented in Figure 4.3, most of the orders failed to be produced on-time (waiting) and with the complete order. An additional analysis showed that the causes from the main problems were the lack of raw material, i.e. steel, production program, production line, and external factors that neither the company nor the CIP team could control (see Figure 4.4).

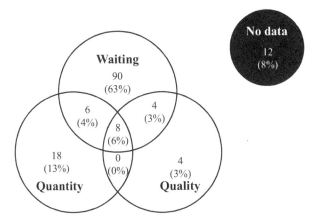

FIGURE 4.3
Division of fulfillment causes in groups
(Adapted from Hidalgo-Chavero et al., 2017)

Combining the information obtained from the previous two analyses, the CIP team observed that 78% of the orders that failed for waiting and quantity failed due to production program problems. Two different approaches were used to identify the root causes: structuring diagram and current reality tree (CRT). A structuring diagram was used to identify root causes from a soft system perspective, obtaining three causes: lack of process standardization (each sales order is communicated differently), the activities per area are not properly defined, and lack of alerts to send a sales order at the right time. After discussing these findings with the organization's employees, they validated the "lack of process standardization" as the main root cause. This root cause included symptoms such as excessive use of emails to communicate information between departments and the presence of human errors in different activities (e.g. the conversion of metrics/units and manual determination of due dates).

The CRT and "five-whys" were used for a hard (production) system perspective, observing four main root causes, namely: there was not an alert system to notify when a process was complete, employees did not work together, the labeling system was not user friendly, and the warehousing management control was not effective. Some of the symptoms grouped in these root causes were that forklift operators did not know when to move reels from one machine to another, the data displayed on the label on reels was small and difficult to read from the forklift seat, and the lack of communication between employees from different departments (including frontline employees).

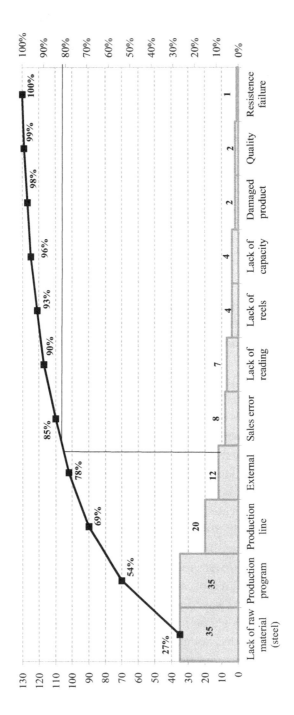

FIGURE 4.4

Pareto diagram of the fulfillment causes subgroups
(Adapted from Hidalgo-Chavero et al., 2017)

Using an interaction process between the CIP team members and CIP facilitator, five unique activities were grouped into two main solutions (see Tables 4.1 and 4.2). Three of the main contributions from this

TABLE 4.1

Solution A: System design to improve information flow

Root cause addressed	Actions	Benefits
Lack of standardization of processes, each order is carried out differently	Excel application	- Decrease probability of human mistakes by hand calculations - Waste activities removed - Trustworthy information registration
Lack of standardization of processes, each order is carried out differently Employees do not work together	Weekly meetings	- Improvement of internal communication between administration and the manufacturing plant - Analysis of failures and feedback - Solution proposals

TABLE 4.2

Solution B: Warehouse controls

Root cause addressed	Actions	Benefits
Lack of standardization of processes, each order is carried out differently and employees do not work together	Weekly meetings	- Improvement of internal communication between administration and the manufacturing plant - Analysis of failures and feedback - Solution proposals
The labeling system is not user friendly	Finished product labels redesigned	- Forklifts operators do not need to get off the truck to check the labels - Security risks and errors are reduced
There is not an alert system that notifies when a process is completed Lack of alerts to send and order at the right time	Andon system	- The forklift operators do not waste time looking for who needs their services - Improvement in flow of communication between manufacturing line and forklift operators
Lack of standardization of processes, each order is carried out differently and the warehousing control is not suitable	Steel requirement by system	- Delivery time reduction for all raw materials - Distance and time reduction - Elimination of daily stock take

feedback process were: to include weekly meetings between departments involved in the order flow, to create an Excel application to reduce waiting time (instead of the participation of IT department to develop a software application), and the authorization to purchase rechargeable batteries for tablets. Considering that these five activities did not require economic investment to implement, the organization leader approved the implementation of these actions as is documented in the following sub-section.

4.2.2 Phase II: Do

During this step in the PDCA problem-solving methodology, each of the five activities was tested and fully implemented. Excel application (see Figure 4.5) automated the calculations that previously were done by hand and converted the order to the needed units (kilograms, pound, meter, or/and feet) shared between three departments or areas (i.e. Planning, Programming, and Raw Material Purchasing), and documented a promise date of delivery to the customer. This application helped to increase communication between these three different departments.

A weekly meeting was established to discuss on-time delivery failed orders and the reason of these incidences following this agenda, namely: following up previous actions (5 minutes), failed orders and causes (20 minutes), solution designs or Kaizen (20 minutes), next orders vs. inventory (10 minutes), closing meeting (5 minutes). This meeting was designed considering six thinking hats (de Bono, 1985), where each participant contributes

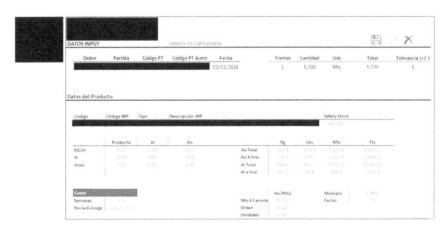

FIGURE 4.5
Excel application
(Part of solution A; obtained from Hidalgo-Chavero et al., 2017)

to the meeting in a different way: white hat (production; objective), green hat (acquirement; creative), black hat (raw material acquirement; negative), red hat (planning and feedback; positive), and blue hat (planning and input; organization), yellow hat (programming: emotional).

Redesign of the finished product identification labels (see Figure 4.6) was an important activity not only because of their impact on the process but also because it was an initiative requested by frontline employees. Forklift operators had to step down from the cockpit and read the labels on the reels and determine the destination. In the best case scenario, the machine operator would tell the driver where to take the material or finished product. By reorganizing the information on the labels used to identify the reels, and making the size of the destination or next step in the process larger, the forklift operators could easily read and quickly identify the place the reel needed to be delivered.

Furthermore, while reviewing the possibility to install an Andon light system, the supervisor mentioned that there used to be a system where machine operators would request reels to feed the wiring machines. These indicated the quantity, time and place from where a machine was comin, after which the forklift driver would see and bring to the corresponding machine. This system allowed the supervisor to monitor the forklift's activity. However, the system was left aside because the tablet that served as a link between the forklift operator and the system itself needed to be taken off to be recharged. To bring the system back online, a brainstorm session occurred, and the simplest, less costly and eligible solution came up, using external batteries to charge the tablet when needed.

Lastly, to improve the annexation of the steel products to the required system needing to be made, the procedure would be like every other

FIGURE 4.6
Finished product label redesign
(Obtained from Hidalgo-Chavero et al., 2017)

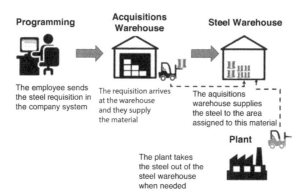

FIGURE 4.7
Raw materials requisitions process
(Adapted from Hidalgo-Chavero et al., 2017)

material (see Figure 4.7). It was necessary to instruct and train the programming department to do the requirements. Once this was done, the warehouse forklifts were instructed to leave the steel reels in a specific area, called the steel patio, where during the day and as needed production forklifts would come and take the correct material.

4.2.3 Phase III: Check

These activities were implemented around week eight of this CIP and monitored during eight more weeks, i.e. 16 weeks of CIP duration in total. The two actions related to system design to improve information flow (solution A) helped to achieve a reduction of 75% in order fulfillment failure by stopping wrong information being fed through the administration channel. On the other hand, the additional three actions taken related to warehouse controls produced two main benefits, namely: a reduction of 96% in muda, i.e. waste, in time spent on activities related to steel products (savings of 109 minutes) and a reduction of 13% of forklifts' travel distance per day (savings of 89 meters per day).

Remembering the general objective of action research, when it started on the first days of June 2016, the indicator of order fulfillment was 90% (see Figure 4.8). On September 2016, the implementation took effect (Do-step) and the indicator rose to 98%, which meant that two orders failed to deliver on-time . Lastly, in October there was only one failure related to on-time delivery.

FIGURE 4.8
Steel orders fulfillment order indicator
(Obtained from Hidalgo-Chavero et al., 2017)

4.2.4 Phase IV: Act

As part of the feedback and learning processes observed during the implementation of the actions, the CIP team conducted the following activities: a procedure describing how to use the Excel application was created and integrated into the organization's ISO 9000 documents. The new finished product label document was also updated (as format/record) in the organization's ISO 900 documents, and job profiles were updated according to the new responsibilities (i.e. weekly meeting roles and completion of the information in the Excel application).

The final step for the project consisted of integrating the steel requirement system made in Excel, into the company's IT system, allowing the order information to be filtered automatically. This would enable a faster and more reliable flow of information between the relevant areas. However, because of the CIP duration scope and the resources needed to be completed, it was not possible to finish this action by the end of the 16 weeks.

4.3 FACTORS RELATED TO CIP SUCCESS

Considering that this CIP was finished on time (i.e. 16 weeks), with a minimum investment (i.e. the case organization only paid for the redesign of the finished product label), and it achieved the initial goal of increasing fulfillment level by 7% (i.e. fulfillment level increased from 88% to 98%), this project could be classed as a successful CIP. From the information described in this case study, there are several factors that could be related to CIP success. These include data availability, target area commitment to change, structured methodology, and goal process definition. However, in order to increase the knowledge about the factors related to CIP success, a survey was applied at the end of the CIP to university CIP team members (see Table 4.3) using a six-point Likert scale (1 = not at all important, 2 = low importance, 3 = somewhat important, 4 = moderately important, 5 = very important, 6 = extremely important).

TABLE 4.3

Factors related to CIP success in case study B

Factors	CIP team member 1	CIP team member 2	CIP team member 3	Mean	SD
Goal development process	6	6	6	6.00	0.00
Team member experience	6	6	6	6.00	0.00
Team autonomy	6	6	6	6.00	0.00
Stakeholder representation	6	6	6	6.00	0.00
Internal team roles	6	6	6	6.00	0.00
External champion/sponsor	6	6	6	6.00	0.00
Team size	6	6	6	6.00	0.00
Team improvement skills	6	6	6	6.00	0.00
General management support	6	6	6	6.00	0.00
Management involvement	6	6	6	6.00	0.00
Management understanding of CI	6	6	6	6.00	0.00
Action orientation	6	6	6	6.00	0.00
Tool appropriateness	6	6	6	6.00	0.00
Structured methodology	6	6	6	6.00	0.00
Goal clarity	6	6	5	5.67	0.47
Software	6	5	6	5.67	0.47
Facilitation	5	6	6	5.67	0.47
Solution iterations	5	6	6	5.67	0.47
CIP technical documentation	6	6	5	5.67	0.47
Goal alignment	6	5	5	5.33	0.47
Problem scope	6	5	5	5.33	0.47
Team member time	5	6	5	5.33	0.47
Support from CI program	6	5	5	5.33	0.47
Planning for institutionalization	4	6	6	5.33	0.94

(Continued)

TABLE 4.3 (*Continued*)

Factors related to CIP success in case study B

Factors	CIP team member 1	CIP team member 2	CIP team member 3	Mean	SD
Target area understanding of CI	5	5	5	5.00	0.00
Target area commitment to change	6	4	5	5.00	0.82
CIP planning	6	4	5	5.00	0.82
Team commitment to change	6	4	5	5.00	0.82
Team communication and coordination	6	5	4	5.00	0.82
CIP progress reporting	6	5	4	5.00	0.82
Data trustworthiness	5	5	4	4.67	0.47
Organizational policies and procedures	4	5	5	4.67	0.47
Organizational culture	4	5	5	4.67	0.47
Organizational structure	4	5	5	4.67	0.47
Target area representation	6	4	4	4.67	0.94
General resource support	6	4	4	4.67	0.94
Materials and equipment	6	4	4	4.67	0.94
Target area routineness	3	5	6	4.67	1.25
Goal difficulty	4	5	4	4.33	0.47
Training	4	4	5	4.33	0.47
Follow-up activities	4	4	4	4.00	0.00
Data availability	5	3	4	4.00	0.82
Cross-functionality	6	3	3	4.00	1.41
Project identification and selection	4	4	3	3.67	0.47
CIP priority	5	3	3	3.67	0.94
Deployment of changes	6	2	3	3.67	1.70
Team harmony	6	2	3	3.67	1.70
Project duration	4	3	3	3.33	0.47
Performance evaluation/review	2	4	4	3.33	0.94
Information from previous CIPs	4	2	2	2.67	0.94
Financial resources	2	2	3	2.33	0.47
Lessons learned	4	1	2	2.33	1.25
Recognition and rewards	1	1	1	1.00	0.00

It is interesting to observe that 14 out of the 53 factors were considered by the three university CIP team members as extremely important (i.e. six-point scale) to achieve CIP success. Seven out of these 14 factors were focused on the team design category (see Chapter 1, Table 1.5), which is made up of nine factors. Only target area representation (mean = 4.67, SD = 0.94) and cross-functionality (mean = 4.00, SD = 1.41) factors were not considered extremely important by the three university CIP team members. This evidence shows that the key for the success of this CIP was highly related to the way in which the CIP team was designed, including factors such as team experience, team autonomy, and internal team roles.

In addition, it is important to highlight that ten out of the 53 initial factors were considered by the university CIP team members as less than moderately important (4-point Likert scale). These mainly related to organizational factors (see Chapter 1, Table 1.6), including factors that referred to the process followed to identify the CIP and the resources needed to conduct it. Finally, although the CIP success would lead to the CIP team members being awarded their ISE bachelor's degree and the possibility of also obtaining a summa cum laude award; they considered recognition and awards as the least important factor in achieving the CIP goal.

4.4 REFERENCES

Bono, E. D. (1985). *Six Thinking Hats*. Boston, MA: Little, Brown.

Cagliano, R., Kalchschmidt, M., Romano, P., & Salvador, F. (2005). EurOMA-POMS Joint International Conference. *Journal of Manufacturing Technology Management*, 16(4). https://doi.org/10.1108/jmtm.2005.06816daa.001.

Checkland, P., & Scholes, J. (1999). *Soft Systems Methodology in Action*. West Sussex, UK: Wiley.

Chung, W., Ching, S., & Saad, S. M. (2007). *Benchmarking: An International Journal: Benchmarking the Management of Operations and Information Systems*. Bradford, GB: Emerald Group Publishing Limited.

Croxton, K. L. (2002). The order fulfillment process. *The International Journal of Logistics Management*, 14(1), 19–32.

Hidalgo-Chavero, M. E., Muñiz, Y. A. S., De León, A. J. C., Aleu, F. G., Vazquez, J., Verduzco-Garza, T., & Lozano, J. A. (2017, January). A continuous improvement project to increase the fulfillment level in a wire and cable company. In *Proceedings of the International Conference on Industrial Engineering and Operations Management*.

Oly Ndubisi, N., & Kahraman, C. (2005). Teleworking adoption decision-making processes: multinational and Malaysian firms comparison. *Journal of Enterprise Information Management*, 18(2), 150–168.

5

Setup Time Reduction in a Packaging Line in the Beverage Industry

5.1 CIP RESUME

Best manufacturing practices are not only about the application and implementation of the latest machineries and technologies, but they must also include a system and management approach. A worldwide beverage manufacturing organization is ruled by the Total Production Maintenance (TPM), using the Operational Production Indicator (OPI) as one of its key production performance metrics. The OPI is the organization's internal name for Overall Equipment Effectiveness (OEE).

Recently, one of the most important production plants of the case company located in the north of Mexico was having problems to achieve the OPI level in some of its six different production lines (called: Production Line 1, Production Line 2, Production Line 3, Production Line 4, Production Line 5, and Production Line 6); especially in Production Line 5. Thus, the main objective of this CIP was to increase the OPI in Production Line 5 by one percentage point. To achieve this goal, two secondary objectives were formulated, namely: reducing the change time in the labeling machine of Production Line 5 by 15% and increasing the availability of Production Line 5 by 1%. In order to achieve the primary and secondary goals, the CIP team used a set of tools that included optimization models, Gemba walk, time study, Pareto diagram, single minute exchange of die (SMED), and Ishikawa diagram under the umbrella of the Lean problem-solving methodology.

The analysis showed that the main causes of increases in stoppage time due to change of a product's presentation in the production line were due to production planning, which only considered Material Requirement Planning, instead of also taking into account the operating restrictions.

Additionally, the lack of updating the operative documents referring to the product change procedures negatively impacted the correct execution of the production operations on the shop-floor. The design of a solution to the problem included a model of optimization for the production sequence based on the theory of the Travelling Salesman Problem, where the cost was considered as the time of change between the runs. Also, the change procedures were standardized, by updating the operative documents (i.e. manuals, One Point Lesson and standard operation sheets). Using the 5's methodology, visual aids were installed for the correct calibration of the machines, as well as the locations of tool and components. In the same way, the development of a system of periodic updating of the operational documents was promoted. The results of the optimization of the production sequence showed an average increase of 14 working hours per month, i.e. a decrease of 30% in the time of unemployment per presentation. Additionally, the execution of the standardized change procedure significantly reduced rework, the latter representing 20% of the total time of change in the most expensive machine. Both solutions had an impact (one with a 2% increase in the OPI) achieving the CIP goals.

This CIP was developed over 16 weeks in the fall of 2018 by five CIP team members (one CIP leader/facilitator, three university CIP team members, and one organization CIP team-member), spending a total of 1,241 hours in the CIP as follow: CIP leader/facilitator 19 hours and the university CIP team members 1,222 (25 hours per week per member). The organization CIP team member's time was not recorded.

5.2 CIP DESCRIPTION

The problem-solving methodology used in the project is based on the case study: The implementation methodology of lean manufacturing developed by (Halim et al., 2013); which consists of six stages: Plan, Analyze, Design, Implement, Evaluate and Standardize (see Table 5.1).

5.2.1 Stage I – Plan

As it was indicated in Table 5.1, the goal of stage 1 (Plan) was to select the process or system to be improved. In order to achieve this goal, the CIP team members followed five steps:

TABLE 5.1

Problem-solving methodology

Methodology stages	Activities/Methods Applied
Plan: Select system to be improved	• Understanding of the process • Description of need • Cost of unemployment • Objectives • Interview with the client
Analyze: Study the existing system	• Process analysis and data collection: line observation (Gemba walk), time study, mapping the current system, and identify waste • Root cause analysis
Design: Design improve system	• Current situation • Simulation of the process • Expected benefits • Impact on the general objective
Implement: Improvement/ kaizen activities	• Time study • Measure existing system • Set-up time reduction
Evaluate: Review improved process	• Time study of the new system • Result evaluation: productivity analysis and cost saving analysis
Standardize	• Standardized Work

a) **Understanding the process:** The project was carried out on Production Line 5, which works with non-returnable bottles of 325 ml and 355 ml. Production Line 5 was operated by 25 workers, 24 hours a day, seven days a week; manufacturing six different beverage brands, mainly for exporting to the international market (96%). The manufacturing process followed in Production Line 5 consisted of six steps. First, during the depalletizing step, new bottles are moved from the pallet to the conveyor belt. Second, bottle inspection is the step where bottles with defects or contaminated with dirt are removed from the production line. Third, during the filling step, clean bottles are filled and the lid is placed on. Fourth, the pasteurizing step is focused on controlling the risk of contamination of the product with pathogenic microorganisms. Fifth, if the product manufactured in Production Line 5 requires a label (some bottles do not need a label as the bottle is engraved), then this is pasted on during the labelling process. Sixth, according to the product presentation format, the bottles are packed. Lastly, boxes are placed on a pallet for storage and transportation.

b) **Description of need:** To calculate the efficiency and effectiveness of the packaging lines, the beverage manufacturing organization uses an Operational Performance Indicator (OPI). The main problem present at Production Line 5 was that it was not fulfilling the goal of the OPI, mainly due to the stoppages that appeared on the line. The OPI goal for Production Line 5 was 82.8% OPI points in 2017, but the actual figure obtained was 81.3 % OPI points.

c) **Cost of unemployment:** The average cost per line stop was $444 dollars per hour, which included energy used, maintenance, and labor. From January to August of 2018, there was a cost of $315,000 dollars due to stoppages in Production Line 5. From this amount, $135,000 dollars corresponded to production line stops generated due to changes in the presentation of products.

d) **Objectives:** As it was mentioned during the previous section of this chapter, the CIP team members defined the main objective of this CIP as gaining one percentage point on the OPI on Production Line 5. To achieve this goal, two secondary objectives were formulated, namely: reduce the change time in the labeling machine of Production Line 5 by 15% and increase the availability of the Production Line 5 by 1%.

e) **Interview with the client:** After the initial diagnostic conducted during the Plan stage of the problem-solving methodology, the CIP team members conducted several meetings with clients (i.e. Plant manager and Production Line 5 Leader). The meetings allowed the CIP team to validate that the project was aligned to the beverage manufacturing organization's strategic plan, that the CIP goals satisfied their needs, and to obtain authorization to access any information from the line during the 16 weeks of the CIP.

5.2.2 Stage II – Analyze

The analysis stage of this problem solving-methodology consisted of understanding the cause–effect relationships of the conditions that existed within the packaging line 5. The actions that were carried out in the analysis stage included historical data collection and production line observations.

On average, Production Line 5 produced 920,009.58 hectoliters in 2017, using 62 different SKUs (presentations). Only 4% were sold in the national market; while 96% were exported to the international market. Products for the international market had different requirements according to the country where they would be sold. For example, product requirements were different for Canada and the United States. This situation generated an increase in the number of stock keeping unit (SKU). Through an analysis of the volumes of each SKU, it was identified that 78% of the production in this line was mainly focused on two SKUs (SKU1 = 71% and SKU2 = 7%).

Furthermore, as it was mentioned early, in 2017 there was a gap of 1.5% between OPI results (81.3%) and OPI goal (82.8%) in Production Line 5. Historical data from 2017's OPI in this line (see Figure 5.1) showed important improvement opportunities in changeover operations, breakdowns, and external stops.

With the main objective of identifying symptoms related to change over time, breakdowns, and external stops, over the course of a week the CIP team members observed the three-shifts available in Production Line 5 and interviewed the 25 front line workers from this line. Findings from this activity were documented as five main symptoms:

a) Excessive changeover of the filling machine. Production Line 5's capacity was defined by means of the filling machine, which processed 750 bottles per minute. The goal that the case beverage

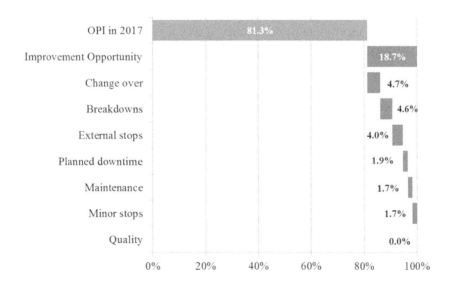

FIGURE 5.1
2017 Production Line 5 OPI

organization was pursuing was to achieve 100% efficiency during 100% of the time. This meant that the total of the bottles that reached the end of the line should not be different from the capacity of the filling machine. For sanitary reasons, a cleaning on-site had to be carried out, when there was a product brand change. Cleaning on-site included mechanical and chemical processes that were essential for the hygiene of the food process. This was carried out without having to disassemble the system. Therefore, the CIP team was not allowed to intervene in this process.

b) Excessive changeover in the labelling machine. In 2016, the marketing team launched a new round label for exported bottles (formerly square). This had had an impact on increasing changeover times. Until mid-2018, 10 changes were made every 7 days, whereas currently, 2 changes were made every 7 days. Each change had an average duration of 54 minutes due to the main adjustments that were made to the machine.

c) Lack of raw material inspection. Bottles, labels, and boxes were not inspected in the warehouse after they were received from the supplier as they had a quality certification from the supplier. This decision was made due to the high demand for the materials. To verify that these materials would not affect the change times, label samples were collected in the raw material warehouse and in the production line. After carrying out rub and plan tests in the beverage manufacturing organization's quality laboratory, it was determined that there were no significant variations in the specifications of the labels. However, it was identified that both the OPL (One point Lesson) manuals and the Standard Operation Sheet of the labelling machine were outdated. It was also observed that the materials used for square and round labels were not identified, so when the changeover was made it generated confusion since they were very similar.

d) Excessive changeover in packing machine. After carrying out a time and motion study in the packing train, it was identified that the workers took an average of 45 minutes to make the changeover for the product presentation of 12, 18 and 24 bottles. Additionally, a sample of 30 observations was collected from the beverage manufacturing organization database for each change between product presentations in order to identify if there was any significant difference in any particular changeover (see Table 5.2). However, there was not a significant difference between the various product presentations.

TABLE 5.2

Classification change packaging train

Changes of presentation	Stoppage time (minutes)
12-18 pack	41.27
18-24 pack	39.20
12-24 pack	42.33
24-18 pack	40.59
24-12 pack	41.09

e) Poor production program development. At the moment of the present study, 17 SKUs were manufactured per week, covering a variety of 28 weekly presentation changeovers on average. Table 5.2 shows the most frequent changeovers that occurred in Production Line 5. As it was mentioned early, SKU1 had the highest production volume in this line and represented 11% of the total possible changeovers (2,396 total changes). When analyzing the production plan that was created weekly, the following findings were identified: the production sequence was repetitive, whereas the production plan was created based only on the MRP system. For example, the same SKU could appear up to 5 times in different production times.

Considering the five findings or symptoms obtained from the observation of Production Line 5, the CIP team members called for a meeting with front line workers and developed an Ishikawa diagram to determine the root cause of the problem "Low OPI level in Production Line 5". In addition to the initial five findings, front line workers contributed by mentioning 16 more symptoms; all the 21 symptoms were developed using the 5-why's technique. After finishing the Ishikawa diagram, two root causes were validated and selected, namely: "there is not an optimal production sequence" and "there is no standard procedure for updating operational documents".

5.2.3 Stage III – Design

Three improvement actions were developed to eliminate the two root causes: "there is not an optimal production sequence" (improvement action #1) and "there is no standard procedure for updating operational documents" (improvement actions #2, #3, and #4):

a) Create an optimization model of the production sequence of SKUs (improvement action #1). The characteristics of the model included the following criteria: using Excel Solver add-in, generate all possible sequences, choose the sequence with the minimum stoppage time, be fed from a database of estimated times, and be fed from a real database. To develop this optimization model, the CIP team used the Travelling Salesman problem variations model (Johnson & McGeoch, 2007). The reliability of the model depends on the accuracy and representativeness of the change times stored in the database compared to the operational reality of the production line. That is, the change time used to run the model should realistically represent the production line's changeover times. The model worked in the following way: a matrix of change times was generated with the SKUs that were going to be manufactured. Then, by means of the Solver tool, the target of decreasing time was selected, the restrictions for the sequence variations were established and the model was solved. Considering that the model used an asymmetric matrix, it was recommended to solve the matrix through the Evolutionary method. It took 30 seconds to solve a problem with 16 variables, on average. In order to obtain the expected benefits from the model, a sample of 4 weeks was divided in two different scenarios, this was done in order to see the impact regardless of the seasonality of the year (see Table 5.3).

b) Standardize the changeover process by updating the operation production line (OPL) manuals and the standard operation sheet (improvement action #2). In order to reduce the changeover time, the OPL manuals and the Standard Operation Sheets of the Labeling and Packing Train area were updated.

c) Give front line workers access to OPL manuals and standard operation sheets (improvement action #3). In order for front line workers

TABLE 5.3

Simulation of the production sequence model

Performance metrics	Impact on high demand	Impact on low demand
Time reduction	761.8 minutes	2,507 minutes
Bottles produced	571,372	1,880,250
OPI improvement	1.81%	5.96%

to have easy access to these documents, the CIP proposed placing tablets with QR codes on the floor.

d) Implement visual aids in the areas or processes needed (improvement action #4). Labels were created to mark all the zones and tools needed by the front-line staff during a changeover.

5.2.4 Stage IV – Implement

Improvement proposals were assessed by the client during the CIP team follow up meetings. Considering that the entire set of proposals would be finished during the remaining time of the CIP (6 weeks) and these proposals did not represent a high financial investment, the client approved the four proposals. Results from the implementation of these proposals were as follow:

a) Create an optimization model of the production sequence of SKUs (improvement action #1). The model of sequence optimization of production had a significant impact on the weeks with the greater amount of SKU because this involved more presentation changeovers. The 46th week of 2018 (week 15 of the CIP) was the one selected for the implementation of the model; this was the last week available before the end of the project. During week 46th, the tentative production sequence for Production Line 5 was released, taking into account the theoretical operating restrictions, and compared with the optimization model production sequence. After introducing the SKUs in the optimization model of the production sequence, the reduction of stoppage time due to changeover for presentations was 528 minutes, less than similar weeks from 2017 (see section 5.2.5).

b) Standardize the changeover process by updating the operation production line (OPL) manuals and the standard operation sheet (improvement action #2). To maintain the use of the optimization model, the CIP team trained Production Programmer staff in the use of the optimization model and updated the working procedure, documenting the steps to follow in order to generate every week the new production sequence. This working procedure was included as part of the beverage manufacturing organization quality system.

c) Give front line staff access to OPL manuals and standard operation sheets (improvement action #3). After uploading the updated documents to the central document management platform, the QR codes for each document needed was created and placed on the floor in order to give the front line workers access to these documents using a personal tablet. One electronic tablet per workstation or process was provided (depalletizer, inspection, filler, pasteurizer, labeler, packing, and palletizer). The CIP team conducted a training session with all the front-line workers from Production Line 5 with the objectives of notifying documents updates, the appropriate use of the electronic tablets and the functioning of the QR codes.

d) Implement visual aids in the areas or processes needed (improvement action #4). Some of the activities that front line staff developed during a change SKU required to conduct mechanical modifications in the production line using different equipment and tools. However, the equipment and tools were not identified, consuming unnecessary time from the front-line staff at the moment of performing changeover activities. Therefore, the CIP team designed and implemented visual aids in working floor (see Figure 5.2) based on the work from Kogyo (1996), Meyers & Stephens (2006), and Santos et al. (2006).

5.2.5 Stage V – Evaluate

At the beginning of this CIP, one main CIP goal and two secondary CIP goals were defined: to increase one percentage point on the OPI in Production Line 5 (main CIP goal), to reduce by 15% the change time in the labeling machine of Production Line 5 (secondary CIP goal) and increase the availability of the Production Line 5 by 1% (secondary CIP goal). During this stage of the problem-solving methodology, the CIP team assessed the level of achievement of these CIP goals.

As it was previously mentioned, the deployment of the optimization model for the production program sequence was implemented in the last week of the CIP; therefore, there was no additional time to monitor and assess the effectiveness of this improvement action. However, the CIP team members conducted several simulations with the optimization model using historical data from 2017 and 2018 (see Table 5.3). At the end of week 46 of 2018, the OPI obtained from Production Line 5 was 75. These results did not achieve the OPI annual goal of 82.6%, it is important to compare results from 2018 week 46 with similar weeks from 2017 in order to assess the impact of the optimization model in the OPI level. Table 5.4 shows that comparing three weeks from 2017 with a similar number of

Before	After

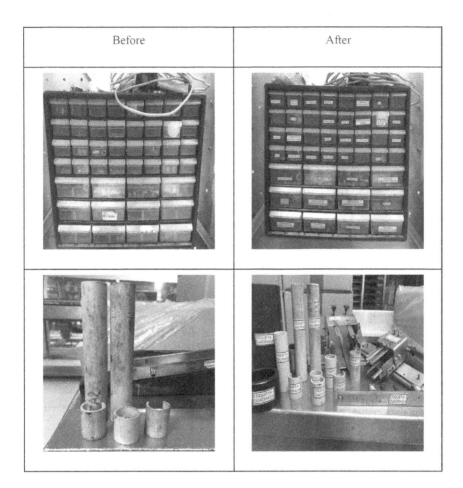

FIGURE 5.2
Visual aids in floor

SKUs, the optimization model helped to improve by 2.7% the OPI level; exceeding the initial main CIP goal of 1%.

As for the secondary CIP goals, the visual aids implemented had an important impact reducing the changeover time in the labeling machine from 54 minutes to 32 minutes (reduction of 40%); exceeding the initial secondary CIP goal of 15%. In addition, with the implementation of the optimization model for programming production sequence, the changeover time was reduced from 758 minutes to 528 minutes (reduction of 30%), increasing the availability of Production Line 5 to manufacture more products and exceeding the secondary CIP goal of increasing the availability of the line by 1%.

TABLE 5.4

Comparison of results from similar weeks in number of SKUs versus week of implementation

Year	Week	No. SKUs	OPI	Changeover (min)
2017	14	17	64%	504
2017	25	16	73%	670
2017	40	16	80%	1100
	Average 2017		72.3%	758
	2018 week 46 (15 SKUs)*		75%	528
	Gap		+2.7%	-230

*Week of the optimization model implementation

5.2.6 Stage VI – Standardize

In addition to the training provided by the CIP team members to front line workers and the documentation of the new procedures in the central document management platform during the implementation of the improvement actions, two activities were developed to close this CIP. First, the CIP was documented in an executive report and delivered to the client. Second, the CIP team conducted a meeting with middle-level managers and the production plant manager to describe all the activities, findings, and solutions performed during the CIP.

5.3 FACTORS RELATED TO CIP SUCCESS

Considering that this CIP was finished on time (16 weeks), with a minimum investment (organization only paid for the redesign of the finished product label), and achieving its goals, this CIP could be classed as a successful CIP. From the information described in this case study; there are several factors that could be related to CIP success. These include data availability (historical data), target area willingness to change, structured methodology, goal process definition, and tools appropriateness (optimization models). However, in order to increase the knowledge about the factors related to CIP success, a survey was applied at the end of the CIP to university CIP team members (see Table 5.5) using a six-point importance Likert scale (1 = not at all important, 2 = low importance, 3 = somewhat important, 4 = moderately important, 5 = very important, 6 = extremely important).

TABLE 5.5

Factors related to CIP success

Factors	CIP team member 1	CIP team member 2	CIP team member 3	Mean	SD
Target area commitment to change	6	6	6	6.00	0.00
Team member time	6	6	6	6.00	0.00
Data availability	6	6	6	6.00	0.00
Data trustworthiness	6	6	6	6.00	0.00
Team commitment to change	6	6	6	6.00	0.00
Team harmony	6	6	6	6.00	0.00
Action orientation	6	6	6	6.00	0.00
Tool appropriateness	6	6	6	6.00	0.00
Goal development process	6	5	6	5.67	0.47
Goal clarity	6	5	6	5.67	0.47
Goal alignment	5	6	6	5.67	0.47
Team autonomy	6	5	6	5.67	0.47
Internal team roles	6	5	6	5.67	0.47
Team size	6	6	5	5.67	0.47
Team improvement skills	5	6	6	5.67	0.47
Organizational culture	6	6	5	5.67	0.47
Team communication and coordination	6	5	6	5.67	0.47
Structured methodology	6	5	6	5.67	0.47
External champion/sponsor	6	5	5	5.33	0.47
General resource support	6	5	5	5.33	0.47
Materials and equipment	6	5	5	5.33	0.47
Facilitation	5	5	6	5.33	0.47
Organizational policies and procedures	5	6	5	5.33	0.47
Follow-up activities	6	5	5	5.33	0.47
Lessons learned	5	5	6	5.33	0.47
Solution iterations	5	5	6	5.33	0.47
Target area routineness	6	4	6	5.33	0.94
Target area understanding of CI	6	4	6	5.33	0.94
Team member experience	6	4	6	5.33	0.94
Software	6	6	4	5.33	0.94
CIP planning	5	5	5	5.00	0.00
CIP priority	5	5	5	5.00	0.00
Problem scope	5	4	6	5.00	0.82
Information from previous CIPs	6	5	4	5.00	0.82
Performance evaluation/review	5	6	4	5.00	0.82

(Continued)

TABLE 5.5 (*Continued*)

Factors related to CIP success

Factors	CIP team member 1	CIP team member 2	CIP team member 3	Mean	SD
Organizational structure	6	4	5	5.00	0.82
Planning for institutionalization	5	4	6	5.00	0.82
CIP progress reporting	6	3	6	5.00	1.41
Goal difficulty	5	4	5	4.67	0.47
Management understanding of CI	5	4	5	4.67	0.47
Stakeholder representation	5	3	6	4.67	1.25
Training	6	3	5	4.67	1.25
CIP technical documentation	5	3	6	4.67	1.25
Project duration	4	4	5	4.33	0.47
General management support	4	4	5	4.33	0.47
Project identification and selection	5	3	5	4.33	0.94
Support from CI program	5	3	5	4.33	0.94
Deployment of changes	4	3	5	4.00	0.82
Target area representation	5	5	2	4.00	1.41
Management involvement	4	3	4	3.67	0.47
Financial resources	6	3	2	3.67	1.70
Cross-functionality	5	3	2	3.33	1.25
Recognition and rewards	5	3	2	3.33	1.25

It is interesting to observe that eight out of the 53 factors were considered by the three university CIP team members as extremely important (six-point scale) to achieve CIP success. Four factors were focused on the CIP process (see Chapter 1 Table 1.5), i.e. team harmony, team commitment to change, action orientation, and tool appropriateness. Three out of these eight factors were focused on the organization category (see Chapter 1 Table 1.6), i.e. data availability, data trustworthiness and team members time. Lastly, one factor was focused on the task design category (target area commitment to change).

Ten additional factors were rated as extremely important by two out of the three CIP team members who assessed them with a six-point score. In this set of factors, there are a predominant number of them focused on the team design (four factors), task design (three factors), CIP process (two factors), and organization (one factor) categories. Overall, considering factors with a mean between 6.0 and 5.67, it could be assumed that factors focused on the CIP process (six out of ten factors), task design (four out of nine factors), and team design (four out of nine factors) were critical to CIP success by the CIP team members.

On the other hand, it is important to highlight that four out of the 53 initial factors were considered by the CIP team members as less than moderately important (4-point Likert scale); mainly related to organizational factors (Chapter 1, Table 1.6). Also, it is important to mention that cross-functionality was a factor with a low score, although the CIP team needed to include in this CIP front line workers and production programmers. Finally, although the CIP success meant university CIP team members could obtain their ISE bachelor's degree and the possibility of a summa cum laude award; they considered recognition and awards as the factor with the lowest impact in achieving the CIP goal.

5.4 REFERENCES

Halim, N. H. A., Jaffar, A., Noriah, Y., & Naufal, A. A. (2013). Case study: The methodology of Lean manufacturing implementation. *Applied Mechanics and Materials*, 393, 3–8.

Johnson, D. S., & McGeoch, L. A. (2007). Experimental analysis of heuristics for the STSP. In G. Gutin, & A.P. Punnen, *The Traveling Salesman Problem and Its Variations* (pp. 369–443). Boston, MA: Springer..

Kogyo, N. (1996). *Visual Control Systems*. Portland, OR: Productivity Press, E.U.A.

Meyers, F., & Stephens, M. P. (2006). *Diseño De Instalaciones De Manufactura Y Manejo De Materiales*. Mexico City: Pearson Education.

Santos, J., Wysk, R. A., & Torres, J. M. (2006). *Improving Production with Lean Thinking*. Hoboken, NJ: John Wiley.

6

Material Waste Reduction in the Food Industry

![segment break]

6.1 CIP RESUME

To become and remain competitive, organizations must be proactive by focusing on maximizing productivity and achieving quality at the lowest possible cost and at a faster rate than their competitors. To achieve this, organizations use various continuous improvement approaches, e.g. Lean and Six Sigma, to improve their process line performance (Kumar et al., 2006; Snee, 2010; Thomas et al., 2009). Each continuous improvement approach achieves continuous improvement through their own perspective, focusing on and applying different problem-solving methodologies and tools. Antony (2011) describes Lean as a group of tools and techniques to reduce lead times, inventories, set up times, equipment downtime, scrap, rework, and other wastes in a company's operations. On the other hand, Six Sigma is a business improvement approach that seeks to identify and eliminate the causes of defects and variation in business processes by focusing on outputs that are critical to customers (Antony, 2011). Lean Six Sigma (LSS) is a business improvement strategy and problem-solving methodology, based on DMAIC, which improves process performance, resulting in a positive impact on customer satisfaction and obtaining bottom-line results or critical process to generate financial savings (Dora & Gellynck, 2015; Salah et al., 2010; Snee, 2010).

The Lean, Six Sigma, and Lean Six Sigma methodologies have played a significant role in the food industry as a business approach to improve production processes in terms of waste and variability reduction as well as productivity gains. Competitiveness in the food industry can rise through the reduction of waste and lead times through CIPs. This explains the steady growth in the number of researchers and practitioners that have implemented Lean Six Sigma in this sector (Costa et al., 2018; Dora et al., 2014; Mahalik and Nambiar, 2010). Kovach & Cho (2011) propose that product and process alignment can be accomplished by the consistency between five principal elements in the food industry, namely: consumer expectations, expected quality attributes, process control, equipment capability, and commodity specifications. A variation on any of the components could result in consumer disappointment, product holds, ambiguous quality expectations, missing or wrong process checks, increase of waste, downtime in production, consistency issues, and/or decrease in profitability (Hung & Sung, 2011; Kovach & Cho, 2011).

A large food manufacturing organization located in the north of Mexico with 17 unique production lines was having difficulties with the level of raw and process material waste in its confectionary production line. The purpose of this CIP was to reduce the annual kilograms (kgs) of material waste by 21.60% (23,952.42 kg). Considering the characteristics of LSS mentioned previously, the CIP team decided to conduct a Lean Six Sigma CIP project using the DMAIC as the problem-solving methodology. This CIP was developed over 16 weeks in the fall 2018 by five CIP team members (one CIP leader/facilitator, three university CIP team members, and one organization CIP team-member). 962 hours were spent in total in the CIP as follow: CIP leader/facilitator 19 hours and the university CIP team members 943 (20 hours per week per member). The organization CIP team member's time was not recorded.

6.2 CIP DESCRIPTION

CIP team members conducted a Lean Six Sigma CIP project using the DMAIC problem-solving methodology. This provided clarity in each of the five phases of the CIP as follows: (Alsaffar & Ketan, 2018; Antony et al., 2012; Hakimi et al., 2018):

a) The **Define** phase aimed at identifying the process that required improvement as well as determining its scope and objectives.

b) The **Measure** phase involved an assessment of the current state of the process and translating the situation into a measurable parameter that could be used to monitor the achieved improvements.

c) The **Analyze** phase focused on the identification of the root cause(s) that affected the established parameters' behavior.

d) The **Improve** phase consisted in the design, prioritization, and implementation of solutions for the elimination of the root causes of problems selected during the analyze phase.

e) The **Control** phase aimed at standardizing and continuously monitoring the improved methods for sustained results.

By employing this sequential approach, the application of Lean and Six Sigma tools and techniques throughout the project depended on which stage of DMAIC was taking the course. The following sections explain each phase of the study and its results.

6.2.1 Define Phase

CIP team members had an initial project meeting with the food organization management leader to identify the needs for a CIP. After discussing the organization's process performance metrics, CIP team members and manager leaders agreed to delimit the CIP (project scope) to the confectionary production line; which contributed to 26% of the waste cost. The goal of the project was determined to be the reduction of material wasted in the confectionery production line without reducing production volume levels.

In order to quantify the CIP goal, the CIP team used historical data and applied the entitlement equation:

$$CIP\ goal = Baseline - ((Baseline - Entitlement) * 0.7) \qquad \text{(Ec. 6.1)}$$

"Baseline" referred to the average of the existing performance, whereas "Entitlement" considered the best performance achieved during a certain amount of time (historical data from January 2018 to May 2019). In this case, the average material waste per week was 1,362.64 kg and the best performance (minimum material waste) achieved was 701 kg. By substituting these values in formula 6.1, the objective was calculated as follows:

$$CIP\ goal = 1,362kg - ((1,362kg - 701kg) * 0.7) \qquad \text{(Ec. 6.2)}$$
$$CIP\ goal = 1,362kg - 462.7kg = 899.3\ kg \qquad \text{(Ec. 6.3)}$$

With this objective, the CIP project attempted to achieve a reduction of 462.7 kg per week (23,952.42 kg annually), representing a 21.60% decrease. In other words, the CIP main goal was to reduce the kgs of material waste by 21.60% (i.e. 23,952.42 kg).

After defining the CIP's main goal, the CIP secondary goals were also formulated. The 21.60% reduction was divided into the three types of material waste, namely: (1) raw material, (2) semi-finished product, and (3) package. Raw material represented 66.35% of the baseline, while semi-finished product constituted 15.8%, and packaging 17.81%. As a consequence, from the annual objective of 23,952.42 kg of material waste reduction: 15,892.71 kg (14.3% out of 21.6%) corresponded to raw material; 3,794.10 kg (3.4% out of 21.6%) referred to semi-finished products, and 4,265.61 kg (3.9% out of 21.6%) was to packaging.

With the CIP goals defined, the implications in financial and human resources needed to complete these CIP goals were discussed with manager leaders of the food company. They agreed to offer support from the production line supervisor and quality engineering department. Also, any financial requirement from the potential improvement actions would be evaluated by the manager leaders.

6.2.2 Measure Phase

Once the CIP goals were identified, the sampling plan was established. Considering a total of 240 hours (i.e. confectionery production line working hours per week), as well as the desired margin of error of 95%, and confidence rate of 8%, the sampling size calculated resulted in 93 hours of observations through Gemba walks and collection of relevant data. The initial outcome from the Gemba walks was the creation of the confectionery production line SIPOC diagram (see Figure 6.1) to enhance the understanding of the processes involved in this CIP. This included the identification of 12 different SKUs produced in the confectionery production line using six different flavors.

While doing Gemba walks various details of the process were discovered, for example, the origin points of waste, and accumulation of archives about the waste that contained non-value added information.

Therefore, CIP team members conducted the following activities to have an accurate representation of the confectionery production line's current state:

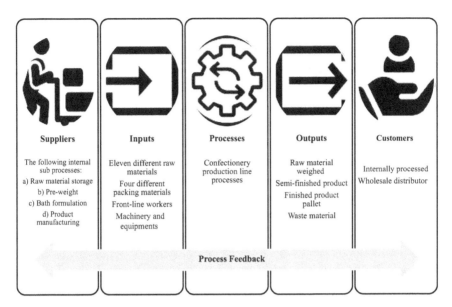

FIGURE 6.1
Confectionery production line SIPOC diagram

- Records updated. CIP team members considered the following actions to update waste data collection records: deletion of redundancies, simplification of contents by removing elements that were not needed or did not add value to the document, standardization of measurement units, and integration of these records in the front-line daily activities.
- Measure raw material wasted in the processes of Pre-Weighing and Formulation. The accumulation of raw material waste was originated principally in three critical zones or areas of the process, namely: raw material dosage, elevator equipment, and mixer machines.
- Measure raw material dosage. This activity was created to understand the raw material dosage application in the batch formulation and product manufacturing process (see Figure 6.1). Observations showed that there was not a standardized procedure that determined how much and when raw material needed to be deposited into the machine.
- Measure raw material in packing. This activity helped to identify packing waste into two categories: those that arrive in a state of non-compliance of quality standards and those that became waste due to

the process. The team discovered that 54% of packing materials were originally sent to the confectionery production line without satisfying the organization's standards of quality, making them unable to be utilized in the manufacturing process. Though it was not used in the process, it was registered as waste for the production line because workers only had one bin to dispose the waste off, consequently disposing both types of waste together and impeding the quantification of each of them.

Findings from the observations and actions conducted during this step of the DMAIC problem-solving methodology were crucial to obtain trustworthy data for the analyze phase.

6.2.3 Analyze

From the 12 SKUs produced in the confectionery production line, six different flavors were used (A, B, C, D, E, and F). Amongst the 6 different flavors of final products, flavors A and B represent 85% of production.

A first approach followed by the CIP team members was to identify whether the flavor ingredient was affecting the level of material waste; therefore, a hypothesis test was conducted to assess if the flavor itself increased material waste. Null and alternative hypotheses were formulated respectively as follows: mean material waste per day is equal for each flavor (Ho) and mean material waste per day is different at least in one flavor (Ha). Considering that the number of days where products with flavors C to F were limited ($n < 10$), then the CIP team decided to test this hypotheses using flavors A and B. With a p-value greater than 0.05 (p-value = 0.936), the CIP team accepted the null hypothesis (i.e. mean material was per day is equal for flavor A and B).

Considering that there was not a difference in material waste due to the flavor used, then the CIP team proceeded to identify which type of material was contributing to the highest amount of waste. This was done by using a kilogram Pareto diagram (see Figure 6.2) and US dollars Pareto diagram (see Figure 6.3). Although, "raw material 1" and "raw material 2" had a significant contribution in the kilograms of material waste, "packing material 1" was the material waste that it was costing more the organization. Additionally, semi-finished material waste had an important contribution to the material waste kilograms and material waste US dollars. Thus, this CIP focused on these four kinds of material waste.

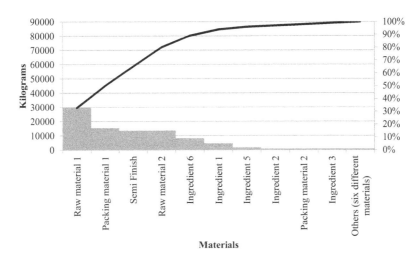

FIGURE 6.2
Kilogram Pareto diagram

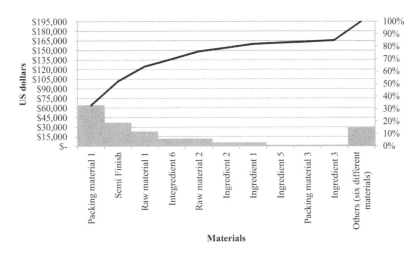

FIGURE 6.3
US dollars Pareto diagram

Knowing this information, the CIP team approached the confectionery product line front line workers to brainstorm ideas with the aim of identifying the causes of waste of raw material 1, raw material 2, and packing 1. These ideas were then used to conduct a Cause-and-Effect analysis to identify the root causes (see Table 6.1). Each one of the root

TABLE 6.1

Root causes per type of material

No	Root causes	Type of material waste	Type of Kaizen
1	There are no adjustment parameters in the process	Semi finished	Kaizen event
2	Pallets with "semi-finished" are not covered with plastic accordingly, not letting the gum cool	Semi finished	Just do it
3	Material handling by operators is not appropriate	Semi finished	Kaizen blitz
4	There is no standard for the reprocess of "raw material 2"	Raw material 2	Kaizen event
	Leakage of "raw material 1" in machinery	Raw material 1	Kaizen event
6	Leakage of "raw material 2" in machinery	Raw material 2	Just do it
7	The design for the recovery of "raw material 2" is not appropriate	Raw material 2	Out of CIP scope
8	"Packing 1" does not comply with quality standards arriving from the supplier	Packing 1	Kaizen event

causes identified were classified by type of material waste and type of Kaizen (i.e. just do it or Kaizen event). These findings were presented in a follow-up meeting with the management leadership team and all the members agreed to remove any actions related to the root cause seven because the design for the recovery of the "raw material 2" would require a large financial investment. Therefore, this root cause was not addressed through this CIP.

6.2.4 Improve Phase

The following action was to determine an implementation plan of the selected solutions, which would then be prioritized considering the required time of implementation, complexity, and impact (Khan, 2006). The root causes were divided into four categories in the Analyze phase, as expressed in Table 6.1, i.e. "out of the project's scope", "just do it", "Kaizen blitz", and "Kaizen event". The following subsections describe the actions conducted to eliminate the root causes classified as just do it, Kaizen blitz, and Kaizen event.

6.2.4.1 Just Do It

"Just do it" are improvement actions where front line workers have the autonomy to decide, implement, and coordinate improvement actions between teams or departments with little or no authorization from the top management (Kato & Smalley, 2012). The CIP team identified three root causes that could be solved using just do it actions:

a) Pallets with semi-finished products were not covered with plastic in the correct way, not letting the gum cool down. This was caused because workers fully covered the semi-finished pallets with plastic wrap, reducing the temperature of the semi-finished product, which produced a deformation of this material in the next step of the production process. The solution, in this case, was to specify in the standard operating procedure (SOP) until which point the pallet should be covered with plastic wrap. With this, the plastic would cover only half of the trays that carry the gum in a pallet. This enabled the semi-finished product to be sufficiently cool for the next step in the process. It also guaranteed that the trays would stay in place (see Figure 6.4). This solution reduced the waste of semi-finished products from 509.29 kg to 219.91 kg on average every week, accomplishing savings of 290.38 kg that represent about USD $820.47. The projected annual savings were 15,099.85 kg, equivalent to USD $42.664.22. The CIP secondary goal in semi-finished waste was to be reduced to 4,265.61 kg; therefore, this CIP exceeded this goal by 354%.

b) Leakage of "raw material 2" in machinery. The function of "raw material 2" was to prevent the semi-finished product getting glued into the machinery. Before the project started, the industrial hopper and a hose in the jigger machine had leaks, causing "raw material 2" get spilled on the floor, converting this raw material into waste. The solution was to weld the industrial hopper edges and to change the jigger machine hose with a new one.

6.2.4.2 Kaizen Blitz

Kaizen blitz is a team-based rapid improvement approach in a specific process (Cox et al., 1995). Traditionally, this type of improvement is performed in one or two days. A Kaizen blitz was performed to eliminate the root cause of semi-finish material waste caused by operators when not

FIGURE 6.4A
Semi-finished product pallet before improvement

FIGURE 6.4B
Semi-finished product pallet after improvement

handling it correctly. This root cause was directly linked to how workers retrieved the product for its later reprocessing and employees from four different departments (i.e. safety, quality, maintenance, and production) were involved. The Kaizen blitz team figured out three solutions, i.e. placing a bin for the reprocessing of semi-finished product at the end of the packing line, determining the necessary quantity of bins for reprocessing, and placing a mark in the bins that showed the maximum filling height.

Bin areas were delimited and the type of bin was determined for each spot depending on the material being disposed of. White cylindrical bins were used for SF, light grey rectangular bins were dedicated for labels and trash in general, and dark grey cylindrical bins were considered for "packing 1". Dark grey cylindrical bins in area 2 were assigned for "packing 1" that did not comply with the organization's quality standards and were unusable for the process, while the same type of bins that were located in area 3 were utilized for the "packing 1" that became waste during the process. The impact of this Kaizen blitz in the CIP goal was not able to be measured directly due to lack of initial data to establish a baseline.

6.2.4.3 Kaizen Events

Kaizen event is "a focused and structured improvement project, using a dedicated cross-functional team to improve a target area work, with specific goals, in an accelerated timeframe" (Farris et al., 2008, p. 10). This approach was used to eliminate the remaining four root causes as follows:

a) There was no adjustment of parameters in the process. Before this project's implementation, there were no parameters for the machinery that processed semi-finished products. As a consequence, there was no control on "raw material 2" usage. To solve this, meetings with front line workers and maintenance personnel were conducted and parameters for vibrator frequency and industrial hopper tube height were defined.

b) There was not a standard procedure for the reprocessing of "raw material 2". Two actions were taken to eliminate this root cause: a machine cover was placed on hopper 1 to prevent leakage and modify reprocess plates' hoppers to assure that "raw material 2" was collected in its entirety. This first action not only reduced "raw material 2" waste but also prevented it invading the packing area, which had caused problems before. For the second action, the team observed that all plates had hoppers, except one. Thus, a major area of opportunity to reduce "raw material 2" waste was found.

c) Leakage of "raw material 1" in machinery. To solve this root cause, maintenance personnel and workers from the line were involved. In this way, people with a technical understanding of the equipment and workers that fully knew the critical points of the machinery worked together to solve this problem. The main sources of leakage were identified as defective seals on the machinery (nine years without being changed) and inactive vibrator on the administration equipment (that helped "raw material 1" fall into the machinery instead of on the machinery and its surroundings). The solutions consisted of changing the seals on the machinery and reactivating the vibrator of the administration equipment. The CIP team decided to install the seals on just half of the machinery to prove that it worked before changing all of them. Verifying the seals' state was also added to the preventive maintenance checklist, with the goal of changing them after a set period of time.

d) "Packing 1" did not comply with quality standards arriving from the supplier. Employees from five different departments (i.e. maintenance, quality, warehouse, commercial, and production) worked to eliminate this root cause with the following actions: set a physical space to separate the two types of "packing 1" waste, create a line on the computer system to charge waste to the supplier, and give back unusable "packing 1" to the supplier for its reprocessing. Before the first action was implemented, workers from the line could not separate "packing 1" that was originally in a bad state (poor quality) because there was only one bin to deposit waste. Thus, an area for a new bin was assigned. The second action modified the manner in which information on "packing 1" was collected. A new entry was added, to differentiate the unusable "packing 1" from the ones becoming waste from the process, in the waste register files. This enabled the confectionery production line to grade the suppliers and to take actions if one was found to be out of the determined range of acceptance. To achieve the third action, the organization reached an agreement with the supplier to receive unusable "packing 1" to reprocess it, achieving a win-win situation.

Additional actions were implemented in the control phase of the DMAIC cycle to maintain these improvement actions in place and quantify the process improvement impact and the percentage of CIP goals achieved.

6.2.5 Control

The confectionery production line had a metric for waste based on levels of performance, called the Daily Floor Management System (DFMS). Before the CIP was carried out, the DFMS did not track waste. Now waste in the confectionery production line was tracked by using two metrics: kg and percentage of waste (the waste in kg/the production in kg). The following controls were developed and utilized to keep track of the process' performance with the implementations that were done:

a) Line up confectionery production line leader with front line workers. A performance board was designed to be placed in the line for it to be seen by the workers at any time. It contained a table that showed the waste goals for the four most critical performance components and the real quantity of waste generated. The board was designed in such a manner that the components were like stickers that could be put on and removed, depending on the components that were critical at any specific moment.

b) Line up confectionery production line leader with organization manufacturing leader. Before the project, the confectionery production line leader registered waste in an Excel file. There was a file for every day of the year for every SKU produced in the day (at least 365 files existed) and with no useful information such as space for signatures, Ishikawa diagram, and waste graph in national currency. As part of the project, a new file was designed with fewer elements on it so that it was user-friendly and easy to fill in. These files were put inside folders for each month of the year so that it was easy to locate them. The file was protected so that the confectionery production line leader could only fill in the cells that were needed (date, leader's name, SKU, production, and waste column). It also had two *poka-yokes*: 1) if the production was not filled in, the performance against the goal was not calculated, and 2) if the SKU was not filled in, the description of it was not shown.

c) Organization manufacturing leader with the management leadership team. Maintenance, quality, safety, production, industrial engineering, and planning personnel participated in daily meetings. Before this project, a board to track these meetings already existed. Nevertheless, it principally focused on corrective actions needed to be done on that specific day because of machine failures or lack of personnel. In other words, the system was not working as it should, considering that its objectives were to show global results of the production line (KPIs), to identify deviations from the business objectives and to establish actions and people responsible for them. In response, a new board was designed. It contained the different KPIs for the organization, including the one for waste broken down into the type of raw material wasted. The approach taken to measure the waste indicator was also modified because it confused the personnel. Before, this indicator was measured by dividing the cost of the material by the kilograms produced in a certain period of time. Later, it was calculated by dividing the kilograms of material wasted by the kilograms of material produced. In this manner, a greater understanding of material waste was obtained.

d) Preventive maintenance checklist. As mentioned in the Improve phase, the machinery needed seals to avoid "raw material 1" leaks. Nonetheless, even when preventive maintenance was carried out weekly, the checklist did not have a task to verify if these seals were still working. After the implementation, this task was added and the seals were verified so that they were replaced if any leakage was detected. Besides this, to ensure that no more "raw material

TABLE 6.2

Impact of improvement actions

Material waste	Objective (kg)	Expecting annual savings (kg)	Expecting annual savings (US dollars)	Impact (%)
Semi Finished	3,794	15,100	42,664	398
Raw Material	15,892	19,742	20,766	124
Packs	4,265	10,123	28,577	237
Total Waste	23,951	44,964	92,008	188

2" leakage occurred, the task of inspecting critical points of the machinery was added, specifically the industrial hoppers and the jigger machine hose.

e) Standard operating procedure (SOP). The confectionery production line already had an SOP document for the machinery. However, its first and only version was made in July 2018. There were many changes made to it since then, including the improvements made on this CIP. All the steps were verified to remove the unnecessary ones, to modify the ones that needed to be changed and to add the new ones.

Considering that it is a common trend in every system to return to its "old" stage, the CIP team focused on implementing these actions to maintain the improvement actions in place and to monitor the metric performance (material waste). After the implementation of the improvement actions (i.e. just do it actions, Kaizen blitz, and Kaizen events), the following step was to keep measuring the material over four weeks to assess the level of the CIP goals' achievement (see Table 6.2). Taking the average of material waste over four weeks and extrapolating this data for a whole year (52 weeks), the improvement actions implemented helped to exceed the secondary CIP goals and the main CIP goal.

6.3 FACTORS RELATED TO CIP SUCCESS

Considering that this CIP was finished on time (16 weeks), with a minimum investment, and achieving the CIP goals, this CIP could be classed as a successful CIP. From the information described in this case study; there are several factors that could be related to CIP success, such as goal definition process, data availability (historical data), data trustworthiness, follow-up meetings with management leader team, and target area willingness to change. However, in order to increase the knowledge about the factors related to CIP success, a survey was applied at the end of the CIP to university CIP team members (see Table 6.3) using a six-point importance Likert scale (1 = not at all important, 2 = low importance, 3 = somewhat important, 4 = moderately important, 5 = very important, 6 = extremely important).

TABLE 6.3

Factors related to CIP success

Factors	CIP team member 1	CIP team member 2	CIP team member 3	Mean	SD
Goal clarity	6	6	6	6.00	0.00
Problem scope	6	6	6	6.00	0.00
Team commitment to change	6	6	6	6.00	0.00
Tool appropriateness	6	6	6	6.00	0.00
Structured methodology	6	6	6	6.00	0.00
Planning for institutionalization	6	6	6	6.00	0.00
Goal development process	6	5	6	5.67	0.47
Stakeholder representation	6	6	5	5.67	0.47
Cross-functionality	6	6	5	5.67	0.47
External champion/sponsor	6	5	6	5.67	0.47
Team size	5	6	6	5.67	0.47
Team improvement skills	6	5	6	5.67	0.47
Facilitation	6	5	6	5.67	0.47
Team harmony	5	6	6	5.67	0.47
Action orientation	6	6	5	5.67	0.47
Solution iterations	6	5	6	5.67	0.47
CIP technical documentation	6	5	6	5.67	0.47
Goal alignment	6	5	5	5.33	0.47
Target area commitment to change	6	5	5	5.33	0.47
CIP planning	5	5	6	5.33	0.47
Financial resources	6	5	5	5.33	0.47
Team member time	6	5	5	5.33	0.47
Performance evaluation/review	6	5	5	5.33	0.47
General management support	6	4	6	5.33	0.94
Data availability	6	4	6	5.33	0.94
Team member experience	5	5	5	5.00	0.00

(*Continued*)

TABLE 6.3 (*Continued*)

Factors rela ted to CIP success

Factors	CIP team member 1	CIP team member 2	CIP team member 3	Mean	SD
Deployment of changes	5	5	5	5.00	0.00
Team communication and coordination	5	5	5	5.00	0.00
Target area understanding of CI	6	4	5	5.00	0.82
Team autonomy	6	4	5	5.00	0.82
Management involvement	6	4	5	5.00	0.82
Management understanding of CI	6	4	5	5.00	0.82
General resource support	6	4	5	5.00	0.82
CIP progress reporting	6	4	5	5.00	0.82
Target area representation	5	4	5	4.67	0.47
Internal team roles	5	4	5	4.67	0.47
Data trustworthiness	5	4	5	4.67	0.47
Organizational policies and procedures	5	4	5	4.67	0.47
Organizational culture	5	4	5	4.67	0.47
Follow-up activities	4	5	5	4.67	0.47
Goal difficulty	5	4	4	4.33	0.47
CIP priority	5	3	5	4.33	0.94
Project duration	6	2	5	4.33	1.70
Lessons learned	4	4	4	4.00	0.00
Training	4	3	4	3.67	0.47
Organizational structure	5	2	4	3.67	1.25
Information from previous CIPs	5	1	5	3.67	1.89
Project identification and selection	6	1	3	3.33	2.05
Materials and equipment	3	2	4	3.00	0.82
Software	3	2	4	3.00	0.82
Target area routineness	3	2	3	2.67	0.47
Recognition and rewards	3	1	4	2.67	1.25
Support from CI program	2	1	4	2.33	1.25

It is interesting to observe that six out of the 53 factors were considered by the three university CIP team members as extremely important (six-point scale) in achieving CIP success. Four factors were focused on the CIP process (see Chapter 1 Table 1.5), e.g. team commitment to change, tool appropriateness, structured methodology, and planning for institutionalization. Two out of these six factors were focused on the task design category (see Chapter 1 Table 1.6), i.e. goal clarity and project scope.

Seventeen additional factors were mentioned as extremely important as two out of the three CIP team members assessed them with a score of six points in the Likert scale. In this set of factors, there was a predominant number of factors focused on the team design category (five factors), the organization category (five factors), the CIP process category (four factors), and the task design category (four factors). Overall, considering factors with a mean between 6.0 and 5.67, it could be suggested that factors focused on the CIP process (eight out of ten factors), task design (six out of nine factors), and team design (five out of nine factors) were critical to CIP success by the CIP team members.

On the other hand, it is important to highlight that nine out of the 53 initial factors were considered by the CIP team members as less than moderately important (4-point Likert scale); mainly related to organization factors (Chapter 1, Table 1.6). Finally, although the CIP success would lead to the CIP team members being awarded their bachelor's degree in Industrial Systems Engineering and the possibility of also obtaining a summa cum laude award; they considered recognition and awards as the factor with the lowest impact (2.67) in achieving the CIP goal. Actually, the realization of this CIP helped one of the university CIP team members to be hired by the organization.

6.4 REFERENCES

Alsaffar, I. & Ketan, H. (2018). Integration of Lean Six Sigma and ergonomics: a proposed model combining mura waste and a rula tool to examine assembly workstations. *IOP Conference Series: Materials Science and Engineering*, 433(1).

Antony, J. (2011). Six Sigma vs Lean: some perspectives from leading academics and practitioners. *International Journal of Productivity and Performance Management*, 60(2), 185–190.

Antony, J., Gijo, E. V., & Childe, S. J. (2012). Case study in Six Sigma methodology: manufacturing quality improvement and guidance for managers. *Production Planning & Control*, 23(8), 624–640.

Costa, L. B. M., Godinho Filho, M., Fredendall, L. D., & Paredes, F. J. G. (2018). Lean, six sigma and lean six sigma in the food industry: A systematic literature review. *Trends in Food Science & Technology*, 82, 122–133.

Cox, J. F., & Blackstone, J. H. (Eds.). (1998). *APICS dictionary*. Falls Church, VA: American Production and Inventory Control Society.

Dora, M., & Gellynck, X. (2015). Lean Six Sigma implementation in a food processing SME: a case study. *Quality and Reliability Engineering International*, 31(7), 1151–1159.

Dora, M., Van Goubergen, D., Kumar, M., Molnar, A., & Gellynck, X. (2014). Application of lean practices in small and medium-sized food enterprises. *British Food Journal*, 116(1), 125–141.

Farris, J. A., Van Aken, E. M., Doolen, T. L., & Worley, J. (2008). Learning from less successful Kaizen events: a case study. *Engineering Management Journal*, 20(3), 10–20.

Hakimi, S., Zahraee, S. M., & Mohd Rohani, J. (2018). Application of Six Sigma DMAIC methodology in plain yogurt production process. *International Journal of Lean Six Sigma*, 9(4), 562–578.

Hung, H. C., & Sung, M. H. (2011). Applying six sigma to manufacturing processes in the food industry to reduce quality cost. *Scientific Research and Essays*, 6(3), 580–591.

Kato, I., & Smalley, A. (2012). *Toyota Kaizen methods: six steps to improvement*. New York: Productivity Press.

Kahn, S. R. (2006). Business performance through Lean Six Sigma: linking the knowledge worker, the Twelve Pillars, and Baldrige. *Choice: Current Reviews for Academic Libraries*, 43(6), 1055.

Kovach, T., & Cho, R. (2011). Better processes make GOOD EATS: food industry can benefit from lean Six Sigma principles. *Industrial Engineer*, 43(1), 36–41.

Kumar, M., Antony, J., Singh, R. K., Tiwari, M. K., & Perry, D. (2006). Implementing the Lean Sigma framework in an Indian SME: a case study. *Production Planning and Control*, 17(4), 407–423.

Mahalik, N. P., & Nambiar, A. N. (2010). Trends in food packaging and manufacturing systems and technology. *Trends in Food Science & Technology*, 21(3), 117–128.

Salah, S., Rahim, A., & Carretero, J. A. (2010). The integration of Six Sigma and lean management. *International Journal of Lean Six Sigma*, 1(3), 249–274.

Snee, R. D. (2010). Lean Six Sigma–getting better all the time. *International Journal of Lean Six Sigma*, 1(1), 9–29.

Thomas, A., Barton, R., & Chuke-Okafor, C. (2009). Applying lean six sigma in a small engineering company: a model for change. *Journal of Manufacturing Technology Management*, 20(1), 113–129.

7

Critical Success Factors for
Continuous Improvement
Projects: A Multi Case Study

7.1 INTRODUCTION

At this point in the book, four full case studies have been described and
their success factors identified by the CIP teams. These case studies offer
information that it is highly relevant to CIP team members and CIP leaders,
e.g. CIP goal process definition, application of soft and hard improvement
tools, application of different problem-solving methodologies, CIP team
coordination, the relevance of reliable historical data, and relevance of target area commitment to change. Nevertheless, the same information from
these case studies is not enough to narrow the 53 factors related to CIP success, see Chapter 1, into a small set of factors called "critical success factors
for CIPs". Therefore, the purpose of this chapter is to propose an initial list
of "critical success factors for CIPs" which can be considered by CIP team
members and CIP leaders to improve the impact or performance of CIPs.
To achieve this goal, the authors conducted empirical research using information from CIPs conducted by senior Industrial Systems Engineering
students from the Universidad de Monterrey during spring 2019.

7.2 RESEARCH METHOD

There are two primary research questions (RQs) that the authors were
interested in addressing. First, considering that for each of the ISE senior
students that participated in this research this was their first experience

as CIP team member, the authors were interested in answering the question: which are the factors most highly related to CIP success from a CIP team member's perspective (i.e. unit of analysis is each CIP team member)? (RQ1). Second, considering each CIP as a unit of analysis, the authors were interested in contrasting the differences between the ranking of each CIP included in this section of the book (four from previous chapters plus the CIP collected in this chapter). Therefore, the second question to address was: which were the factors highly related to CIP success considering the sample of CIP analyzed in this book section (i.e. unit of analysis is the CIP)? (RQ2). To answer these research questions, the authors followed the following research protocol:

a) **Sample size:** Population size is the total number of ISE senior capstone projects in spring 2019, which will be the unit of analysis (one ISE senior capstone project equal to one CIP). Successful CIPs (sample size) were selected interviewing the CIP facilitator and the two CIP dissertation committee members (see Chapter 2). During the interview, the authors only asked three questions: (1) Did the CIP achieve or exceed its initial goals? (2) Did the CIP team finish the project on time? and (3) Did the CIP exceed its budget? If one of these questions was responded to negatively, then the CIP was considered a "less successful CIP" and hence was removed from this research. Finally, if a CIP was canceled by the CIP dissertation committee member during the 16 weeks, this CIP was considered an "unsuccessful CIP" and also was removed from this research.

b) **Data instrument:** This research was limited to those ISE senior students that conducted their capstone project in spring 2019. A survey with two sections was designed. CIP success definition and factors related to CIP success. The first section of the survey included a definition for successful CIPs using three characteristics (i.e. goals were achieved, CIP was finished on time, and CIP was on budget assigned) and four closed questions (i.e. one for each characteristic and an additional question about the average weekly hours spent on the CIP). The second section consisted of an introduction to the factors related to CIP success and the assessment of the 53 factors mentioned in Chapter 1 using the same six-point Likert importance scale (1 = not important at all to 6 = extremely important).

c) **Data collection:** ISE senior students formed their CIP teams (two or three members per CIP team) and their CIP was approved as detailed in Chapter 2. Each CIP team had to document the case study in a full document format and conference proceeding format, which had to be delivered to the ISE Direct office on the last day of the academic term. Therefore, the last day of the term in Spring 2019, at the moment when each CIP team delivered their documents, the ISE director asked the team to complete the survey described in the previous paragraph.

d) **Data screening:** There were three criteria used to exclude respondents from this research (Hair et al., 2016), namely: a survey with 15% or more of data missing would be removed, a survey with suspicious response patters would be removed, and survey items with 15% or more of data missing would also be removed.

e) **Data analysis:** Three main analyses were conducted. First, Cronbach alpha from the valid responses was calculated (Cronbach alpha > 0.7) to assess the reliability of the responses. Second, descriptive statistics (i.e. mean and standard deviation) using individual responses were calculated and used to rank the level of importance for each factor. Third, individual responses were grouped in each CIP and descriptive statistics (i.e. mean and standard deviation) were calculated and ranked.

Results from the application of this research protocol are shown in the following section.

7.3 RESULTS

This section is split into three topics, namely: identification of valid responses, answer of RQ1, and answer of RQ2. The identification of valid responses includes four out of the five steps of the research protocol (i.e. sample size, data instrument, data collection, and data screening). The other two topics consisted on the analysis of data to answer both research questions: which are the factors most highly related to CIP success from a CIP team member perspective (unit of analysis is each CIP team member)? (RQ1) and which are the factors highly related to CIP success considering the sample of CIP analyzed in this book section (unit of analysis is the CIP)? (RQ2).

7.3.1 Identification of Valid Responses

A total of eleven CIPs were run in the Spring 2019 with 32 ISE senior students (i.e. CIP team members). During the last day of the academic term, CIP students personally delivered their final document to the ISE Director Assistant and she requested they complete the paper survey described in the previous section. Once the surveys were collected, these documents were delivered to the authors, who began with the data screening process:

a) CIP missed. One CIP did not complete the survey (three CIP team members); therefore, there was a 90.9% of response rate (ten out of eleven CIPs). These remaining ten CIPs had 29 CIP team members.

b) CIP facilitator not interviewed. Two CIPs (six CIP team members), under the responsibility of the same CIP facilitator, were removed from this investigation as it was not possible to interview the CIP facilitator; remaining eight CIPs with 23 CIP team members.

c) Less successful CIPs. After having interviewed CIP facilitators and CIP dissertation committee members, two CIPs (five CIP team members) were considered as "less successful" and hence were removed from this investigation; remaining six CIPs with 18 CIP team members

d) Successful CIPs. The CIP facilitators and CIP dissertation committee members (15 CIP team members), six CIPs (with 18 CIP team members) were considered as "successful".

e) CIP survey missing data. Two out of the 18 CIP team members showed 98.1% of fulfilment survey (one out of 53 questions was missed). Therefore no CIP team member survey was removed.

f) Strange answer patterns. Two out of the 18 CIP team members answered their survey using a six-point Likert scale value ("Extremely important") in 98% of the questions. Both CIP team members came from the same CIP. Therefore, the authors decided to remove this CIP from the investigation; remaining five CIPs with 15 CIP team members.

After completing all the data screening process, there were 15 valid responses that involved five different CIPs. These CIPs were conducted in four different manufacturing organizations from three industrial sectors, i.e. food (three CIPs), chemical (one CIP), metal (one CIP). These five CIPs exceeded the initial CIP main goal (see Table 7.1) using different

TABLE 7.1

CIPs main goals before and after

CIP No.	Industry sector	CIP main goal description	Initial value	Final value	Percentage of goal achievement
1	Food	Reduce the annual kg of material waste in 23,952 kg	23,952 kg	44,964 kg	188%
2	Chemical	Increase eight percentage points the demand plan assertiveness for special shipments.	8%	58%	725%
3	Metal	Reduce five percentage points the raw material supply cost per ton	5%	9.1%	182%
4	Food	Increase 23 percentage points the candy productivity line	23%	31%	135%
5	Food	Reduce 24 percentage points the waste cost in packing area	24%	36%	158%

problem-solving methodologies such as Six Sigma (DMAIC), Lean Six Sigma, seven-step process improvement methodology, and plan-do-check-act (PDCA). Considering the impact and professional contributions, the authors decided to create a case study using CIP #1 (see Chapter Six).

7.3.2 RQ1: Which are the factors most highly related to CIP success from a CIP team member perspective (unit of analysis is each CIP team member)?

A total of 15 valid responses from CIP team members were included in this research (three CIP team members per CIP). Using SPSS version 25 the authors ran a Cronbach alpha test, which showed a value of 0.95 (higher than 0.7), passing the reliability test.

The top ten factors related to CIP success (see Table 7.2) were mainly grouped in the task design category and CIP process category. Four out of the nine factors (44%) that were grouped in task design category (see Chapter 1) were ranked in a top ten place, i.e. goal development process, goal clarify, problem scope, and target area commitment to change. On the other hand, four out of the ten factors (40%) that were grouped in CIP process category (see Chapter 1) were ranked in a top ten place: tool

TABLE 7.2

Assessing factors importance to achieve CIP success

No.	Factor	Mean	SD	Ranking
1	Goal development process	5.93	0.25	1
31	Facilitation	5.87	0.34	2
2	Goal clarity	5.87	0.50	3
48	Tool appropriateness	5.73	0.57	4
6	Problem scope	5.67	0.47	5
47	Action orientation	5.67	0.60	6
53	CIP technical documentation	5.67	0.60	7
8	Target area commitment to change	5.60	0.61	8
19	General management support	5.60	0.61	9
49	Structured methodology	5.53	0.88	10
16	External champion/sponsor	5.53	1.02	11
44	Team commitment to change	5.50	1.05	12
18	Team improvement skills	5.47	0.50	13
17	Team size	5.47	0.62	14
52	CIP progress reporting	5.47	0.62	15
4	Goal alignment	5.47	0.81	16
21	Management understanding of CI	5.47	0.88	17
32	Data availability	5.47	1.09	18
38	Organizational culture	5.40	0.61	19
36	Performance evaluation/review	5.40	0.71	20
20	Management involvement	5.40	0.88	21
37	Organizational policies and procedures	5.33	0.60	22
11	Team autonomy	5.33	0.70	23
46	Team communication and coordination	5.27	0.68	24
28	General resource support	5.27	0.77	25
45	Team harmony	5.20	0.98	26
41	Follow-up activities	5.14	0.91	27
10	Team member experience	5.13	0.62	28
27	Team member time	5.13	0.81	29
33	Data trustworthiness	5.13	0.88	30
13	Cross-functionality	5.13	1.02	31
51	Planning for institutionalization	5.13	1.50	32
24	CIP priority	5.07	1.03	33
22	CIP planning	5.07	0.93	34
50	Solution iterations	5.07	1.61	35
12	Stakeholder representation	5.00	1.10	36
15	Internal team roles	4.87	0.88	37
43	Deployment of changes	4.87	0.88	38

(Continued)

TABLE 7.2 (*Continued*)

Assessing factors importance to achieve CIP success

No.	Factor	Mean	SD	Ranking
42	Lessons learned	4.73	1.34	39
23	Project identification and selection	4.53	1.71	40
5	Project duration	4.36	1.17	41
9	Target area understanding of CI	4.33	0.79	42
39	Organizational structure	4.27	1.29	43
14	Target area representation	4.20	2.07	44
3	Goal difficulty	4.14	1.36	45
26	Financial resources	3.80	1.76	46
34	Training	3.67	1.40	47
40	Support from CI program	3.67	1.45	48
29	Materials and equipment	3.33	1.99	49
30	Software	3.33	1.99	50
25	Information from previous CIPs	3.27	1.48	51
7	Target area routineness	3.20	1.17	52
35	Recognition and rewards	2.60	1.58	53

appropriateness, action orientation, CIP technical documentation, and structured methodology. It is important to mention that the remaining two out of the top ten factors came from the organization category (see Chapter 1), i.e. facilitation and general management support. The fact that factors grouped in the team design did not obtain a high ranking captured the attention of the authors; and probably an explanation of this situation is the fact that CIP teams were created by the same ISE senior students. Therefore, they knew beforehand the way in which their CIP teammates work.

7.3.3 RQ2: Which are the factors highly related to CIP success considering the sample of CIP analyzed in this book section (unit of analysis is the CIP)?

A total of eight different CIPs were analyzed in the Part II of this book, i.e. those included in Chapters 3, 4, 5 and four CIPs presented in this Chapter (remember that Chapter Six was called CIP #1 in this Chapter). The overall mean from the eight CIPs was calculated and each factor was ranked (see Table 7.3) using descriptive statistics from each CIP (mean and standard deviation).

TABLE 7.3

Factor importance to achieve CIP success (overall mean)

No.	Factor	Mean	SD	Ranking
48	Tool appropriateness	5.83	0.29	1
2	Goal clarity	5.83	0.24	2
31	Facilitation	5.79	0.23	3
1	Goal development process	5.79	0.33	4
47	Action orientation	5.79	0.33	4
49	Structured methodology	5.67	0.65	6
16	External champion/sponsor	5.63	0.54	7
53	CIP technical documentation	5.58	0.46	8
8	Target area commitment to change	5.58	0.49	9
44	Team commitment to change	5.56	0.68	10
18	Team improvement skills	5.54	0.37	11
19	General management support	5.54	0.55	12
4	Goal alignment	5.50	0.37	13
21	Management understanding of CI	5.50	0.58	14
11	Team autonomy	5.46	0.37	15
17	Team size	5.46	0.50	16
52	CIP progress reporting	5.42	0.43	17
32	Data availability	5.42	0.68	18
6	Problem scope	5.38	0.48	19
27	Team member time	5.38	0.59	20
46	Team communication and coordination	5.38	0.42	21
38	Organizational culture	5.33	0.50	22
20	Management involvement	5.33	0.80	23
33	Data trustworthiness	5.29	0.72	24
50	Solution iterations	5.29	1.26	25
37	Organizational policies and procedures	5.25	0.43	26
28	General resource support	5.25	0.57	27
51	Planning for institutionalization	5.21	1.14	28
15	Internal team roles	5.21	0.69	29
45	Team harmony	5.17	0.75	30
12	Stakeholder representation	5.17	0.78	31
10	Team member experience	5.13	0.58	32
22	CIP planning	5.08	0.62	33
41	Follow-up activities	5.04	0.73	34
24	CIP priority	4.98	0.71	35
36	Performance evaluation/review	4.96	0.82	36
13	Cross-functionality	4.67	0.85	37
9	Target area understanding of CI	4.67	0.58	38
39	Organizational structure	4.58	0.85	39

(Continued)

TABLE 7.3 (*Continued*)

Factor importance to achieve CIP success (overall mean)

No.	Factor	Mean	SD	Ranking
42	Lessons learned	4.58	1.23	40
43	Deployment of changes	4.46	0.73	41
14	Target area representation	4.46	1.36	42
23	Project identification and selection	4.38	0.82	43
40	Support from CI program	4.21	1.19	44
3	Goal difficulty	4.21	0.94	45
30	Software	4.21	1.73	46
5	Project duration	4.17	0.75	47
34	Training	4.08	0.98	48
29	Materials and equipment	4.04	1.61	49
7	Target area routineness	3.79	0.94	50
26	Financial resources	3.67	1.45	51
25	Information from previous CIPs	3.50	1.01	52
35	Recognition and rewards	2.38	1.02	53

Thirty-four out of the 53 factors had an overall mean of five or higher, which indicates that CIP teams considered these factors as very important (five-point Likert scale) to achieve CIP success. These 34 factors included the four categories (see Chapter 1): CIP process (ten out of ten factors), team design (eight out of nine factors), task design (five out of nine factors), and organization (eleven out of 25 factors). However, centering our attention on the top ten factors, the CIP process category and task design category had the highest contribution to CIP success.

Another analysis conducted to identify the factors with the highest impact on CIP success was to identify those factors that showed a mean of six-point Likert scale in five or more of the eight CIPs. Under this criterion, six factors had to be mentioned, i.e. tool appropriateness (six out of eight CIPs), goal clarity (five out of eight CIPs), goal development process (five out of eight CIPs), action orientation (five out of eight CIPs), structured methodology (five out of eight CIPs), and team commitment to change (five out of eight CIPs). These six factors were also included in the top ten list.

It is also important to comment on those factors that were considered less important to achieve CIP success (i.e. below four-point Likert scale; moderately important), namely: target area routines, financial resources, information from previous CIPs, and recognition and awards. Three of these factors were grouped in the organization category.

7.4 SUMMARY

Recent publications on factors related to CIP success have been conducted using the systematic literature review (González-Aleu & Van Aken, 2016) and retrospective survey study (González-Aleu et al., 2018) research methodologies to test the same 53 factors. However, these two research methods could impact on research results by the presence of two main biases (Booth et al., 2016; Groves et al., 2011; Petticrew & Roberts, 2008). Thus, the authors suggest continuing the investigation of critical success factors for continuous improvement projects using other research methods. First, content bias is originated by a researcher's interpretation of literature. For example, during a qualitative systematic literature review about critical success factors for CIPs, the researcher collects or extracts partial text from a publication and classifies this extraction as a factor. After collecting the information from all the publications, the researcher can then assess the importance of factors related to CIP success according to how often the factors (or extraction referring to the factor) are mentioned from the total set of papers. Second, retrospective bias can be present in an investigation when the researcher asks a participant to remember a specific episode or fact that occurred in the past. For example, when the researcher asks a participant to assess the level of importance of a set of factors to achieve CIP success, for a CIP that occurred one or more years ago.

To the authors' knowledge, this is the first research that assesses the 53 factors identified by González-Aleu & Van Aken (2016) using information from ongoing CIPs. Although the information presented in this Chapter cannot be generalized to any type of CIP or any type of organization, initial findings suggest that that the initial 53 factors could be reduced in a smaller set of 34 factors based on the CIP team members' perspective. However, from a practitioner or CIP leader perspective, ten factors are consistently considered critical to CIP success: tool appropriateness, goal clarity, facilitation, goal development process, action orientation, structured methodology, external champion/sponsor, CIP technical documentation, target area commitment to change, and team commitment to change. From authors' perspective, these 10 factors should be called "critical success factors".

7.5 REFERENCES

Booth, A., Sutton, A., & Papaioannou, D. (2016). *Systematic approaches to a successful literature review*. Thousand Oaks, CA: Sage.

González-Aleu, F., & Van Aken, E. M. (2016). Systematic literature review of critical success factors for continuous improvement projects. *International Journal of Lean Six Sigma*, 7(3), 214–232.

González-Aleu, F., Van Aken, E. M., Cross, J., & Glover, W. J. (2018). Continuous improvement project within Kaizen: Critical success factors in hospitals. *The TQM Journal*, 30(4), 335–355.

Groves, R. M., Fowler, F. J., Jr, Couper, M. P., Lepkowski, J. M., Singer, E., & Tourangeau, R. (2011). *Survey methodology*. (Vol. 561). Hoboken, NJ: John Wiley & Sons.

Hair, J. F., Jr, Hult, G. T. M., Ringle, C., & Sarstedt, M. (2016). *A Primer on Partial Least Squares Structural Equation Modeling (PLS-SEM)*. Thousand Oaks, CA: Sage.

Petticrew, M., & Roberts, H. (2008). Systematic reviews: Do they 'work' in informing decision-making around health inequalities? Health Economics. *Policy and Law*, 3(2), 197–211.

Part III

Less Successful and Unsuccessful CIPs

It is easy and comfortable to talk about successful projects, but it is rare to find a person interested in talking about less successful and unsuccessful projects. From the authors' perspective, information collected from experiences in this type of project is as valuable as those from successful projects.

The purpose of Part III is to identify the lack of critical success factors that are highly related to less successful and unsuccessful CIPs. To achieve this goal, the authors conducted four activities. First, considering only CIPs from the last year, a list of less successful and unsuccessful CIPs were identified. Less successful CIPs are those that have one or more of the following characteristics: CIP did not finish on time, CIP did not achieve initial goals, and/or CIP did not past the budget assigned. On the other hand, a CIP that was cancelled by the dissertation committee was considered an unsuccessful CIP. Second, an interview was conducted with CIP facilitators from this CIP. During this interview, the authors asked for CIP information, such as the number of CIP team members and organization where the CIP was conducted. Third, after the interview, the CIP facilitator was asked to complete a survey. This survey is similar to that used in the CIP from Part II of this book. Fourth, CIP facilitators were invited to share secondary data (evidence) of CIP follow up formats, CIP assessment formats, and CIP final document. Fifth, information collected from these CIPs were documented in Chapters 8 and 9.

The following two chapters are structured as follow: introduction, description of less successful CIP, and critical success factors missed that influence CIP outcomes.

8

Less Successful CIPs

8.1 INTRODUCTION

As the authors mentioned previously in the introduction of Part II in this book, CIPs that achieved the initial goal in a time of 16 weeks (unless students decided to begin early) and respecting the budget assigned were considered successful CIPs. Otherwise, the CIP was either considered as less successful or unsuccessful. Part II of this book focused on how successful CIPs were conducted: other examples of successful CIPs can be found in different journals and conference proceedings. However, there is a limited number of investigations about factors related to CIPs success as the one included in Chapter 7.

It is difficult to find academic literature (i.e. journal or conference proceedings) describing less successful or unsuccessful CIPs, as well as the factors related to these negative outcomes. Therefore, the purpose of this Chapter is to increase the understanding of the reader about potential mistakes that could be made in CIPs that results in a less successful project. Unsuccessful CIPs will be addressed in Chapter 9. To achieve this goal, the authors undertook a five-step methodology, namely: identification of CIPs, classification of CIPs, faculty advisor interview and survey, review of material available, and production of a final report.

- **Identification of CIPs.** A list of all the CIPs conducted by Industrial and Systems Engineering senior students from the Universidad de Monterrey during the most recent academic term were identified. The purpose of this activity was to reduce or eliminate retrospective bias, which could be present in investigations where the researcher asks participants to remember situations from the past (Groves et al., 2011). In this case, a total of 15 CIPs were identified from spring 2019, less than six months previous to the data collection.

- **Classification of CIPs**. The 15 CIPs were assigned to 10 different faculty advisors. Using the CIP success definition from the introduction of Part II, the authors asked each faculty advisor to classify their CIPs in one of the three categories. This resulted in nine successful CIPs, two less successful CIPs, and one unsuccessful CIP. The three faculty advisors with less successful CIPs and the unsuccessful CIP were invited to participate in an investigation to determine the factors related to the lack of success in those CIPs.
- **Faculty advisor interview and survey**. A one hour interview was scheduled individually with each faculty advisor. During this interview, the authors described the purpose of this book and the importance of obtaining information from less successful and unsuccessful CIPs and asked them to give an overview of the CIP. Then, the faculty advisor answered a survey about how the lack of each of the 53 factors previously mentioned in this book, see Chapter 1, could affect the success of a CIP. The last step during the interview was to invite each faculty advisor to share some information about the CIP. This information included weekly follow up meetings reports (Figures 2.4 and 2.5), monthly assessments (Figure 2.6), and final CIP writing reports.
- **Review of material available**. The authors read the weekly follow up meetings reports, monthly assessments, and final writing reports. Additionally, data from the interview and survey were analyzed and documented in this Chapter.
- **Production of the final report**. As it was mentioned in the Introduction section, this chapter focuses on CIP reports from the two less successful CIPs identified (Sections 8.2 and 8.3), the analysis of factors related to the lack of CIP success (Section 8.4), and conclusions (Section 8.5). Contrary to the Chapters 3 to 7 of this book, where the information from CIPs was written following the structure of the problem-solving methodology used, each less successful CIP report in this chapter was structured as follows: CIP resume (CIP initial goal, problem-solving methodology used, and CIP goal achievement) and CIP opportunities to improve. The section about factors related to the lack of CIP success (Section 8.2.3 and 8.3.3) integrates data collected from the survey answered by the two faculty advisors. Lastly, all the information was summarized and discussed in the conclusion section.

8.2 LESS SUCCESSFUL CIPs: REDUCTION OF A PRODUCTION LINE STOP CAUSES BY STORAGE

8.2.1 CIP Resume

An automotive manufacturing supplier producing five different product families in 43 production lines registered 1,444 production line stoppages from July 2018 to February 2019. This represented an average loss of 1,469 hours per month. The causes of production line stoppages were classified based on issues that included quality (48%), storage (38%), tools (9%), and maintenance (5%). Although quality issues represented the highest production line problem (i.e. 48%), stoppages due to storage were found in 34 out of the 43 production lines. These stoppages were mainly caused by limited raw material storage capacity and obstructed raw material storage. Due to the significance of the stoppages due to storage issues, the CIP team decided to focus on the reduction of this cause, defining the CIP initial goal as reducing production line stoppage time originating from storage problems by 40%. To achieve this goal, the CIP team used the Seven-steps Process Improvement Problem-Solving Methodology (Harbour, 1994) and determined three main actions. i.e. storage re-distribution based on ABC products, implement a push system and implement a product change policy. In this case, the CIP team was only able to implement the product change policy, whereas the other two actions were designed and simulated. Considering the simulations presented by the CIP team, the CIP initial goal would have been achieved; therefore, since the CIP was not finished on time and there was not a full implementation of the proposed solution, the faculty advisor considered this particular CIP less successful.

8.2.2 CIP Opportunities to Improve

After reviewing the following up meetings, monthly assessment reports, and the final CIP report, the authors found six opportunities to improve:

a) **CIP planning**. According to the CIP authorization process followed at Universidad de Monterrey, CIP teams have two opportunities to present a CIP proposal and receive the necessary approval from the committee (December 2018 and January 2019). Documentation from this CIP showed that the committee rejected the first proposal while the second proposal was accepted with changes. Therefore, the CIP team used time during the first week of the CIP to plan activities that should have been carried out earlier, such as rewrite the CIP proposal and obtain customer approval.

b) **Goal development process**. After reviewing the final CIP report, there was not clear evidence that showed the process followed by the CIP team to determine the CIP goal and validate that it could be achieved based on historical data (i.e. entitlement).

c) **Team improvement skills**. The final CIP report showed that the CIP team used basic tools, such as Pareto diagram, Ishikawa diagram, Spaghetti diagram, and flow diagram. Only simulation was the "advanced" tool applied during the CIP. However, independently to the tools used, there was evidence of conceptual problems in their application. For example, the CIP team mentioned in the final CIP report the steps followed to create the Ishikawa diagram, but there were crucial steps missing, i.e. creating the cause–effect diagram with target area representation, conducting brainstorms, and validating root causes. Another opportunity for improvement was observed in the simulation results, there the CIP team did not share information about probabilistic distributions used and the results documented were based on a three samples.

d) **Data availability**. Because the organization did not have information available of the process under study, the CIP team had to spend one week collecting data.

e) **Data trustworthiness**. Data collected during the analysis phase of this CIP included only one out of the three shifts available in the production line. Therefore, data could not represent the full real situation of the production line. Committee members observed this situation and requested to collect data from the other shifts.

f) **CIP team member time.** An essential requirement for the CIP is that it should be finished in 16 weeks. As we mentioned in incise "a" above, the CIP team used the first week to conduct CIP planning activities; therefore, the CIP team only had 15 weeks in total to complete the project. By collecting data from the following up meetings of the first five weeks, it was observed that the CIP team members spent on average 16 hours per week, which is less than the requirement (25 hours per week). This situation was captured by the committee and documented in the meeting report. Therefore, CIP team members had to increase their number of hours during the remaining eleven weeks of the project. At the end of the CIP, only one CIP team member spent less time than the minimum required (21.5 hours per week) and the other two CIP team members spent 25.5 and 31.3 hours per week respectively. This situation consequently reflected the poor performance and progress obtained.

The following step in this investigation was to compare these six findings with the data collected from the survey answered by the faculty advisor.

8.2.3 Factors Related to the Lack of CIP Success

Factors definitions from Chapter 2 were converted into sentences (i.e. "The CIP was less successful because there was not a CIP goal definition process") and the faculty advisor completed the survey using a six-point Likert survey (1 = Totally Disagree, 2 = Disagree, 3 = Somewhat disagree, 4 = Somewhat agree, 5 = Agree, 6 = Totally Agree).

According to the faculty advisor, she reported being somewhat agreed, agreed, or totally agreed in 22 factors (see Table 8.1). Integrating the

TABLE 8.1

Factors related to CIP lack of success in first CIP

Factors	Faculty advisor survey			Researchers findings	Match
	Somewhat agree	Agree	Totally agree		
CIP goal development process				X	
Project scope	X				
Target area routineness	X				
Target area understanding of CI	X				
Team autonomy		X			
Target area representation		X			
Internal team roles	X				
CIP team improvement skills			X	X	X
Management involvement		X			
CIP planning		X		X	X
Financial resources		X			
CIP team member time			X	X	X
General resource support	X				
Materials and equipment	X				
Data availability	X			X	X

(Continued)

TABLE 8.1 (*Continued*)

Factors related to CIP lack of success in first CIP

| | Faculty advisor survey | | | | |
Factors	Somewhat agree	Agree	Totally agree	Researchers findings	Match
Data trustworthiness				X	
Follow-up activities			X		
Lessons learned		X			
Deployment of change			X		
Team commitment to change			X		
Action orientation		X			
Tools appropriateness		X			
Structured methodology			X		
Planning for institutionalization		X			

results from the CIP documentation (follow-up meetings, monthly assessment report, and final CIP report) and the faculty advisor survey, it was observed that four factors were mainly related to the lack of success of this CIP. These were CIP team improvement skills, CIP planning, CIP team member time, and data availability.

8.3 LESS SUCCESSFUL CIPs: REDUCTION OF SALE OPPORTUNITY IN AN INTERNATIONAL HARDWARE ORGANIZATION

8.3.1 CIP Resume

An international hardware organization with different stores in the north part of Mexico was working with two teams: marketing in-store and sales floor. The marketing in-store team was responsible for having the merchandise on the right shelf, as well as the hall clear. On the other hand, the sales floor team was accountable for customer service.

Sale opportunity is a performance metric used by the marketing in-store team to measure all the product that was not exhibited in the shelf. Between 2015 and 2018 sale opportunity increased by 224% in Mexico. For 2018, the value of sale opportunity represented more than 20 million U.S.

dollars in Mexico. Considering the CIP team's physical location, the CIP scope was reduced to just one store in the north division of the hardware organization, called Store "A". During 2018, Store "A" had a sale opportunity of $8,280 U.S. dollars per week, with 430 open spots, or empty spaces, in the shelf per week. The CIP goal was defined as to reduce the open spots in the shelf per week by 5% (i.e. by 22 spots). The CIP team used the plan-do-check-act (PDCA) problem-solving methodology to achieve the CIP's goal.

After a Cause-and-Effect analysis was conducted and diagram drawn, the CIP team identified three potential root causes, namely: storage management system was not user friendly, there was an error in the configuration of the product reception system, and the marketing in-store team used 7% of their time on other activities that did not correspond to the current job description and responsibilities. An improvement action was formulated and implemented for each root cause respectively, these included a turned radio frequency scanner (pilot test), cyclic counting, and workload reassignment. At the end of the CIP, the CIP team obtained an 11.9% reduction in open spots on the shelf (i.e. 51 spots); exceeding the initial CIP goal.

Although this CIP exceeded its initial goal, it is important to mention that the CIP team (two members) completed the project with a delay of four weeks. Therefore, based on the definition of CIP success, this was considered a less successful CIP.

8.3.2 CIP Opportunities to Improve

After reviewing the following up meetings, monthly assessment reports, and the final CIP report, the authors found six opportunities to improve:

a) **Project scope**. From the beginning of the CIP, the scope was not well defined. Initially, the CIP team planned to address the problem in all the stores in Mexico, then the scope was reduced to the North Division stores, and finally to only one store.

b) **Team member size**. From the 15 CIPs conducted by Industrial and Systems Engineering senior students, there were 12 CIPs with a team size of three members, one CIP with a team size of two members (this CIP), and one CIP with a team size of one member. Therefore, team size could have affected the CIP team performance; resulting in the four weeks' delay.

c) **CIP team members' time**. The CIP team was made up of two members who spent an average of 29.4 and 22.8 hours per week; showing a lack of time spent by one of the CIP team members. In reality, both CIP team members were working in other organizations; however, after the second monthly assessment, one of the CIP team members decided to quit a job and focus 100% on the CIP (CIP team member with 29.4 hours per week).

d) **Team communication and coordination**. After reading the final CIP report, the authors observed a lack of writing communication skills that could also be present during the progress meetings, communicating with the faculty advisor as well as target area employees, and/or CIP customer.

e) **Structured methodology**. Although the CIP team decided to use the plan-do-check-act problem-solving methodology, it was observed inconsistency in the steps and tools used.

f) **CIP progress meetings**. After reviewing the follow-up meetings reports, the authors observed that these records were incomplete; only 12 out of 20 were available. Also, not all the fields in these records were completed. These suggested a lack of consistency during the following up meetings.

The following step in this investigation was to compare these five findings with the data collected from the survey answered by the faculty advisor.

8.3.3 Factors Related to the Lack of CIP Success

Factors definitions from Chapter 2 were converted into sentences (i.e., "The CIP was less successful because there was not a CIP goal definition process") and the faculty advisor completed the survey using six-point liker survey (1 = Totally Disagree, 2 = Disagree, 3 = Somewhat disagree, 4 = Somewhat agree, 5 = Agree, 6 = Totally Agree).

According to the faculty advisor, he reported being somewhat agreed, agreed, or totally agreed in 17 factors (see Table 8.2). Integrating the results from the CIP documentation (follow-up meetings, monthly assessment report, and final CIP report) and the faculty advisor survey, it was observed that four factors to the main cause of the lack of success of this CIP. These factors included project scope, team size, CIP team member time, and structured methodology.

TABLE 8.2

Factors related to CIP lack of success in second CIP

Factors	Faculty advisor survey			Researchers findings	Match
	Somewhat agree	Agree	Totally agree		
CIP goal development process			X		
Goal clarity			X		
Goal alignment	X				
Project scope			X	X	X
Team member experience	X				
CIP team improvement skills			X		
Internal team roles	X				
Team size		X		X	X
CIP team improvement skills	X				
CIP planning	X				
CIP priority	X				
CIP team member time			X	X	X
Team commitment to change		X			
Action orientation	X				
Tools appropriateness	X				
Structured methodology	X			X	X
Solution iterations		X			
Planning for institutionalization	X				
CIP progress meeting				X	

8.4 CONCLUSIONS

The purpose of Chapter 8 was to identify factors related to the lack of CIP success. This aim was achieved by reviewing and contrasting CIP documentation (i.e. follow-up meetings, monthly assessment reports, and final CIP reports) and the faculty advisor survey from two less successful CIPs observed in spring 2019. In the first CIP, the CIP team was not able to implement the solutions and so they were able to validate it only through simulation. Twenty-two success factors were identified, but only four factors were presented in the CIP documentation and the faculty advisor survey, namely: CIP team improvement skills, CIP planning, CIP team member time, and data availability. The second CIP showed that the CIP team spent four more weeks than initially assigned (i.e. 25% more time) and not all the actions were completely implemented. Seventeen success factors were identified, but only four factors were presented in the CIP documentation and the faculty advisor survey, i.e. project scope, team size, CIP team member time, and structured methodology. Integrating the results from both CIPs, it is observed that seven factors (one factor was repeated in both CIPs) could be related to the lack of CIP success, namely: team improvement skills, CIP planning, team member time, data availability, project scope, team size, and structured methodology.

Although the methodology and sample size (two CIPs) could be improved, this chapter offers information that it is not usually available in academic publications or practitioners publications. For practitioners, it is clear that the CIP team members' time is related to the lack of CIP success. This is a factor that CIP leaders need to observe in every step of the problem-solving methodology. On the other hand, from a research perspective, further work should be conducted to determine the consistency or divergence of the findings obtained.

8.5 REFERENCES

Groves, R. M., Fowler Jr, F. J., Couper, M. P., Lepkowski, J. M., Singer, E., & Tourangeau, R. (2011). *Survey Methodology* (Vol. 561). Hoboken, NJ: John Wiley.
Harbour, J. L. (1994). *The Process Reengineering Workbook: Practical Steps to Working Faster and Smarter Through Process Improvement*. New York: Quality Resources.

9

Unsuccessful CIPs

9.1 INTRODUCTION

Unsuccessful CIPs are those CIPs that were halted before the implementation of the improvement actions. In these CIPs, the organization spent employees' time and other resources, without obtaining a positive impact (i.e. improvement) on the performance of the targeted area. As it was mentioned in the previous chapter, it is difficult to find information about documented cases of less successful CIPs, but it is even more difficult to find information about unsuccessful CIPs. Ninety-seven CIPs have been conducted from spring 2015 to spring 2019 at Universidad de Monterrey, and only two have been considered unsuccessful (spring 2016 and spring 2019). Organizations implementing CIPs and practitioners as CIP leaders could obtain valuable insights from research on unsuccessful CIPs; resulting in a better planning, assignation of resources, and ultimately in a better execution of the CIP.

Therefore, the purpose of this chapter is to identify the factors related to unsuccessful CIPs. To achieve this goal, three data collection instruments were used, i.e. faculty advisor interviews, retrospective survey, and historical records analysis. First, the faculty advisor interview consisted of a one hour interview. During this time, the authors described the purpose of this book and the importance of obtaining information from unsuccessful CIPs. This interview aimed to obtain a background, or context, about the unsuccessful CIPs, as well as to bring back faculty advisor memories related to the CIPs. This activity was essential to reduce potential retrospective bias (Groves et al., 2011). Second, the faculty advisor answered a survey about how the lack of each of the 53 factors previously established in Chapter 1 could have affected CIP success. Factors definitions from Chapter 1 were converted into sentences (i.e. "The CIP was less successful because there was not a CIP goal definition process") and the faculty advisor completed the survey using a six-point Likert scale (1 = Totally Disagree, 2 = Disagree, 3 = Somewhat disagree, 4 = Somewhat agree, 5 = Agree, 6 = Totally Agree). Third, CIP reports, or historical records, were read by the authors to triangulate and validate some of the findings (Bailey & Bailey, 2017).

Each unsuccessful CIP is documented in the following sections considering two topics: CIP resume and factors related to unsuccessful CIP. The last section of this chapter, i.e. conclusions, includes an analysis contrasting findings from both unsuccessful CIPs.

9.2 UNSUCCESSFUL CIP: INVENTORY MANAGEMENT IN A SMALL SIZE MANUFACTURING ORGANIZATION

9.2.1 CIP Resume

Small-size and family companies have an important role in creating job opportunities. However, these organizations operate on a daily basis with limited financial resources. Therefore, the correct or smart use of their resources is essential to have a healthy organization. The purpose of this CIP was to design an inventory management system for a small manufacturing organization.

The CIP was conducted by four CIP team members, namely: one university CIP team member (i.e. ISE student), two organization CIP team members, and one CIP faculty advisor. After a recurrent lack of progress at the first CIP progress meeting, the committee decided to cancel the CIP.

9.2.2 Opportunities to Improve Factors Related to Unsuccessful CIP

From the CIP reports or historical data, the authors observed eight factors that drove the faculty advisor and the committee to cancel the CIP:

a) **Goal clarity**. CIP goals should be measurable, but this was not observed in this CIP (see section 9.2.1). Therefore, the CIP committee requested the CIP team to formulate a measurable goal during week 1 of the project.

b) **Project scope**. Considering that there was only one university CIP team member, the committee requests the CIP team member to reduce the scope of this CIP and define measurable goals. The CIP team member decided do not follow this advice.

c) **Team member experience**. This CIP was the first participation of the university CIP team member in a CIP.

d) **Team size**. The CIP was conducted by only one university CIP team member, giving him complete responsibility for the results of the CIP.

e) **Team improvement skills**. Although the university CIP team member had training in different tools and problem-solving methodologies, the two organization CIP team members did not have knowledge on tools and problem-solving improvement methods.

f) **Team commitment to change**. The fact that in several of the CIP progress meetings the university CIP team member did not arrive on time and did not bring his "to do" list was interpreted as a lack of commitment with this CIP.

g) **Tool appropriateness**. Evidence such as the elaboration of an Ishikawa diagram by the university CIP team member showed a lack of correct use of this tool, which raised doubts about his technical knowledge on improvement techniques.

h) **Team member time**. Weekly progress report (see Figure 2.4) showed that the CIP team member dedicated an average of 15 hours per week, when he was expected to spend 25 hours per week or more.

i) **Data availability**. The following facts suggested a lack of data availability: smallorganization, the lack of measurable CIP goal, and the lack of enough historical data to analyze inventory levels in the first CIP progress meeting.

9.2.3 Factors Related to Unsuccessful CIP

On the other hand, after analyzing the faculty advisor survey results, 21 out of the 53 factors were considered as "Somewhat Agree" (4-point Likert scale), "Agree" (5-point Likert scale) or "Totally agree" (6-point Likert scale); impacting in the failure of this CIP (see Table 9.1).

The triangulation process conducted using the faculty advisor's interview, CIP report or historical data, and faculty advisor's survey, suggested that *team member experience, team size, team member skills, team member time, team commitment to change,* and *tool appropriateness* were the six factors most highly related to the unsuccessful CIP.

TABLE 9.1

Factors related to unsuccessful CIPs

Factors	Faculty advisor survey			Researchers findings	Match
	Somewhat agree	Agree	Totally agree		
Goal clarity				X	
Project scope				X	
Target area commitment to change	X				
Team member experience	X			X	X
Stakeholder representation	X				
Internal team roles	X				
External champion/sponsor	X				
Team size			X	X	X
Team improvement skill			X	X	X
Management involvement	X				
Management understanding of continuous improvement			X		
Team member time	X			X	X
Data availability				X	
Follow-up activities	X				
Lessons learned	X				
Team commitment to change		X		X	X
Team harmony	X				
Team communication and coordination	X				
Tool appropriateness	X			X	X
Structured methodology			X		
Solution iterations			X		
Planning for institutionalization			X		
CIP progress reporting		X			
CIP technical documentation		X			

9.3 UNSUCCESSFUL CIP: TRANSPORTATION COST REDUCTION IN AN AUTOMOTIVE MANUFACTURING ORGANIZATION

9.3.1 CIP Resume

Automotive manufacturing organizations have an essential role in the Mexican economy. A European automotive manufacturing organization located in the central part of Mexico was interested in improving their cost-effectiveness and decided to conduct a CIP. The goal of this CIP was to reduce the ground transportation cost per car produced by 10%.

Different from other CIPs mentioned in this book, this CIP was conducted by three CIP team members: one university CIP team member, one organization CIP team member, and one CIP faculty advisor. The CIP team performance decreased over time, obtaining a satisfactory first progress meeting, a disappointing second progress meeting, and CIP cancelation in the third progress meeting (during week 14 out of 16).

9.3.2 Opportunities to Improve

After conducting the faculty advisor interview and reviewing the CIP report or historical data available from this CIP, the authors identified that the lack of the following factors were related to the failure of this CIP:

a) **Team commitment to change**. During the second and third progress meeting, the faculty advisor observed a lack of interest in the university CIP team member to finish the CIP.

b) **Team member time**. The university CIP team member was working full time in the automotive manufacturing organization, but in a different department that the CIP target area, hence no enough time was spent working on the project for the targeted CIP area.

c) **Target area representation**. The organization CIP team member was not highly related to the CIP target area.

d) **CIP planning.** There was observed a lack of research or data collection to validate or define a target area performance baseline previously the initiation of the CIP.

9.3.3 Factors Related to Unsuccessful CIP

On the other hand, after analyzing the faculty advisor's survey results, 34 out of the 53 factors were considered as "Agree" (5-point Likert scale) or "Totally agree" (6-point Likert scale); impacting in the failure of this CIP (see Table 9.2).

The triangulation process conducted using the faculty advisor's interview, CIP report or historical data, and faculty advisor survey, suggested that *target area representation, CIP planning, team member time*, and *team commitment to change* were the four factors most highly related to unsuccessful CIP.

TABLE 9.2

Factors related to unsuccessful CIP

| | Faculty advisor survey | | Researchers | |
Factors	Agree	Totally agree	findings	Match
Goal alignment	X			
Target area routines	X			
Target area commitment to change	X			
Target area understanding of continuous improvement	X			
Team member experience	X			
Team autonomy	X			
Stakeholder representation	X			
Cross-functionality	X			
Target area representation	X		X	X
Internal team roles	X			
External champion/sponsor	X			
Team size		X		
Team improvement skills	X			
General management support	X			
Management involvement	X			
Management understanding of continuous improvement	X			
CIP planning		X	X	X
Project identification and selection		X		
CIP priority		X		
Information from previous CIPs		X		
Team member time		X	X	X
Facilitation		X		
Data availability		X		
Data trustworthiness		X		
Lessons learned	X			
Deployment of change	X			
Team commitment to change		X	X	X
Action orientation		X		
Tool appropriateness		X		
Structured methodology		X		
Solution iterations		X		
Planning for institutionalization		X		
CIP progress reporting		X		
CIP technical documentation		X		

9.4 CONCLUSIONS

The purpose of Chapter 9 was to identify factors related to unsuccessful CIPs. This aim was achieved by reviewing and contrasting CIP documentation (i.e. follow-up meetings, monthly assessment reports, and final CIP reports) and the faculty advisor survey from two unsuccessful CIPs observed in spring 2016 and spring 2019. In the first CIP (Section 9.2.3), the analysis suggested that there were six factors related to the unsuccessful CIP: *team member experience, team size, team member skills, team member time, team commitment to change,* and *tool appropriateness.* In the second CIP (Section 9.3.3) the analysis suggested that there were four factors related to the unsuccessful CIP: *target area representation, CIP planning, team member time,* and *team commitment to change.* Comparing both CIPs, *team member time,* and *team commitment to change* are a common denominator in the unsuccessful CIPs. This finding could be interpreted as the lack of *team member time* and *team commitment to change* could produce an unsuccessful CIP.

9.5 REFERENCES

Bailey, C. R., & Bailey, C. A. (2017). *A guide to qualitative field research.* Thousand Oaks, CA: Sage.
Groves, R. M., Fowler, F. J., Jr, Couper, M. P., Lepkowski, J. M., Singer, E., & Tourangeau, R. (2011). *Survey methodology* (Vol. 561). Hoboken, NJ: John Wiley.

10

Summary

10.1 INTRODUCTION

A key element of Performance Excellence models is the application of continuous improvement initiatives through all the organization's processes, such as CIPs. Some of the most popular CIPs used in manufacturing and services organizations are Kaizen events, Lean Six Sigma projects, Six Sigma projects, and general quality improvement projects (i.e. plan-do-check-act or plan-do-study-act, Six Sigma, and Lean Six Sigma). In the previous chapters, we have provided evidence of CIPs and established some of the potential reasons and factors for their successful and unsuccessful execution. In this chapter, we summarize the most important finds or contributions obtained in each Part of this book (sections 10.1 to 10.3). Then three additional subsections were included to address critical success factors for CIPs (see section 10.4), limitations of the findings documented in this book (see section 10.5), and recommendations for future work (see section 10.6).

10.2 SUMMARY PART I – CONTINUOUS IMPROVEMENT PROJECTS OVERVIEW

There are five main ideas that readers would be able to capture from this chapter. First, there are different types of CIPs (i.e. Kaizen events, Lean Six Sigma projects, Six Sigma projects, general quality improvement projects, etc.). Second, CIP success can be measured using soft metrics (i.e. CIP team member or stakeholders' perceptions) and hard metrics (i.e. target area performance metrics, percentage of goal achievement, etc.). Third, the most extensive list of factors related to CIP success consist of 53 factors grouped into four categories: task design (see Table 1.3), team design (see Table 1.4), CIP process (see Table 1.5), and organization (see Table 1.6). Each of these tables includes factor name and definition. Four, universities conducting industrial and systems engineering senior projects have a gold mine in which to conduct and study the impact of CIPs in organizations, as well as the opportunity to improve local businesses. Five, the book documents how a Mexican university is using and managing their senior projects to conduct CIPs, which could be an important source of information to practitioners to conduct continuous improvement initiatives.

10.3 SUMMARY PART II – SUCCESSFUL CIPs

Each of the successful CIPs included in Chapter 3 to Chapter 6 showed that CIP initial goals were exceeded on-time and within the assigned budget (if there was one). Also, these CIPs showed the utilization of different problem-solving methodologies. Additionally, the authors highlight below four best practices identified from these successful CIPs:

a) **System thinking**. CIP team members used a mapping process and input-process-output diagram (see Figure 3.1) to describe the current state of an Emergency Medical Service (EMS) organization. Other tools used by the CIP teams to represent systems were the rich picture (see Figure 4.1), the turtle diagram (Figure 4.2), and supplier-input-process-output-customer (SIPOC) diagram (see Figure 6.1). These tools helped the CIP team members to obtain a better understanding of the process under investigation.

b) **Cause-effect analysis**. The identification of real root causes is critical to eliminate negative effects that are not desired. From the authors' perspective, the Ishikawa diagram is the most frequently used tool to identify the root causes of problems; but this tool is also often misused, for instance, critical steps that include the development of the tool through a team working session and asking "why?" five times in each initial symptom are often skipped. This situation is observed in several academic publications. In Chapter 3, the CIP team used the current reality tree (see Figure 3.2) to identify the root cause of the problem. This tool was developed by Eliyahu Goldratt, and its construction is based on the collection of symptoms and the identification of a cause and effect relationship between symptoms. Another example of the importance of a good cause and effect analysis is observed in Chapter 5, where the CIP was initially born as a Single Minute Exchange Die (SMED) project, but the root cause obtained was a lack of production program procedure.

c) **Hands-on**. Chapter 4 and Chapter 6 show us that advance statistical analyses are not always necessary to obtain outstanding achievements. Achievement of CIP goals are perhaps more related to CIP team members' hands-on action. In these two chapters, CIP teams conducted several Kaizen events and just-do-it actions to solve the problem detected.

d) **CIP unconventional tools**. A traditional mind set for practitioners leading or participating in CIPs is to apply basic tools and metrics (i.e. Pareto diagram, Ishikawa diagram, dispersion diagram, value steam-map, mean, standard deviation, etc.), middle level complexity tools (i.e. control charts, correlations, test hypothesis, etc.), and in some cases, advanced tools (i.e. design of experiments, multivariate analysis, etc.). However, there are unconventional tools that practitioners could use to obtain outstanding results such as geographic analysis (see Chapter 3) and optimization modeling (see Chapter 5). The geographic analysis helped the CIP team to identify the best place to relocate ambulances and the optimization modeling helped the CIP team to define the best production sequence.

Chapter 7, the last one in Part II, focused on identifying the factors related to CIP success by analyzing several CIPs. CIP leaders and CIP team members should be focused on ten factors to conduct a successful CIP, i.e. tool appropriateness, goal clarity, facilitation, goal development process, action orientation, structured methodology, external champion/sponsor, CIP technical documentation, target area commitment to change, and team commitment to change.

10.4 SUMMARY PART III – LESS SUCCESSFUL AND UNSUCCESSFUL CIPs

There is a lack of information about less successful CIPs and unsuccessful CIPs; usually, organizations are not willing to share this information. Evidence of lack of success in different company's initiatives could damage their branding. However, these CIPs are an essential source of information to improve CIP effectiveness. As a CIP leader and CIP team member, it is important to identify the lack of which factors could produce a less successful and unsuccessful CIP. In addition, from a research perspective, it is important to identify these factors to validate, or complement, the list of the ten critical success factors mentioned previously (see section 10.2).

Collating information collected from interviews, surveys, and historical records, the authors agreed that the lack of the following factors could produce less successful CIPs (see Chapter 8): team improvement skills, CIP planning, team member time, data availability, project scope, team size, and structured methodology. The lack of the following factors could produce an unsuccessful CIP: target area representation, CIP planning, team member time, and team commitment to change.

10.5 CRITICAL SUCCESS FACTORS FOR CIPs

Integrating the list of factors related to CIP success (Chapter 7), the lack of factors related to less successful CIPs (Chapter 8), and the lack of factors related to unsuccessful CIP (Chapter 9), a total of 17 factors were grouped (see Table 10.1) as follows: four factors in task design category, four factors in the team design category, five factors in the CIP process category, and four in the organization category. These factors are recognized by the authors as "critical success factors (CSFs)." Comparing the information in Table 10.1 to Tables 1.3 to 1.6, it is observed that a high proportion of the CSFs came from the task design (four out of nine; 44%), team design (four out of nine; 44%), and CIP process (five out of ten; 50%) categories. Therefore, CIP leaders and CIP team members have to put special attention to CSFs in these three categories.

TABLE 10.1

Critical success factors

Classification	Factor	Definition	Chapter 7	Chapter 8	Chapter 9
Task design	Goal development process	Development of goals by CIP team members during the project	X		
	Goal clarity	Extent to which CIP goal (s) are clear to CIP team members and stakeholders	X		
	Problem scope	Size and nature of the problem addressed by the CIP, in terms of number of employees, physical space, organizational processes and functional boundaries, and breadth of problem areas targeted		X	
	Target area commitment to change	Commitment of target area employees to change	X		
Team design	Target area representation	Representation of target area employees on CIP team			X
	External champion/sponsor	Support, guidance, and approval provided by champion(s)/sponsor(s) external to CIP team	X		
	Team size	Number of people directly participating as members of CIP team		X	
	Team improvement skills	Team members' knowledge and skills in problem-solving, improvement, and change management methodologies and tools		X	
CIP process	Team commitment to change	CIP team members' commitment and accountability to improve the target area and to achieve CIP goals	X		X
	Action orientation	Extent to which CIP team has a focus on action including data collection, experimentation/testing and implementation	X		

(Continued)

TABLE 10.1 *(Continued)*

Critical success factors

Classification	Factor	Definition	Chapter 7	Chapter 8	Chapter 9
	Tool appropriateness	Appropriateness of problem solving and improvement tools used to analyze and solve problems	X		
	Structured methodology	Extent to which improvement methodology is systematic, well-defined, and executed thoroughly	X	X	
	CIP technical documentation	Documentation and dissemination of information to stakeholders on goal achievement, changes made to processes (new procedures), data and findings, other outcomes, and recommendations	X		
Organization	CIP planning	Activities documented before CIP launch to plan and coordinate the CIP (e.g., team member selection, goal definition, arranging resources, data and document gathering, etc.)		X	X
	Team member time	Ability of CIP members to allocate necessary time needed for the project		X	X
	Facilitation	Facilitation, guidance, and coaching available to improvement Project team throughout the Project	X		
	Data availability	Access for CIP to data needed for the Project		X	

10.6 LIMITATIONS

Although this book was not focused on conducting rigorous research about CIPs and generalized the results to any type of CIP in organizations, the authors decided to use practical research or case studies using qualitative methodologies (i.e. historical data and interviews) and quantitative methodologies (i.e. data from CIPs and surveys) to collate information and increase the body of knowledge for CIP leaders, CIP team members, and researchers interested in this topic. Readers should be aware that the information collected in this book has the following limitations: number of CIPs (sample size) and data source collection (only CIPs from higher education in the north part of Mexico).

10.7 FUTURE WORK

From a practitioner (i.e. CIP leaders and CIP team members) and researcher perspective, the next step should be focused on monitoring these 17 factors in every CIP to increase the impact of the improvement actions on the targeted area. On the other hand, from a researcher perspective, efforts should be concentrated in two areas. First, conduct extensive research collecting CIP team member perceptions to measure the relationship between these 17 CSFs on CIP success. Second, the Shingo model, a performance excellence model, says that "ideal behaviors" produce "sustainable results." Therefore, a list of "ideal behaviors" should be created for each CSF and test their importance to achieve the CIP goal and maintain CIP results.

Index

Note: Page numbers in italic and bold refer to figures and tables, respectively.

A

"Act" phase, 65
Ambulance response times
  analysis phase, 41–46
  CIP resume, 37–38
  cycle times, 39
  design and implementation phase,
    47–48
  pre-diagnostic phase, 38–41
  results phase, 48–49
  success factors, 49–50
  turnaround times, 39, 44
"Analyze"/"Analysis" phase, 41–46, 72–75,
    87, 90–92
Andon light system, 63
Antony, J., 85
Approval of CIPs, 27–29
Assessment of CIPs, 31–32
Automotive manufacturing, 118–122,
    130–132

B

Beverage industry *see* setup time in a
    packaging line
Brainstorms, **44–46**
Budgets, 4

C

Case studies
  ambulance response times, 37–52
  critical success factors, 103–112
  importance of, 23
  inventory management, 128–130
  material waste reduction, 85–101
  order fulfillment levels, 55–68
  production line stoppages, 118–122
  sale opportunity reduction, 122–125

setup time in a packaging line, 69–83
  transportation costs, 130–132
Cause-and-Effect analysis, 91–92, 123,
    136–137
Champions, **10**
Change
  deployment, **17**
  target area commitment to, **8**, 18,
    107, **139**
  team commitment to, **11**, 18, 111–112,
    129, 131–133, **139**
Changeover times, 73–74, 77,
    79, **80**
"Check" phase, 64, *65*
Cho, R., 86
CIPs *see* continuous improvement
    projects (CIPs)
Classification of CIPs, 4–5, 118
Closing of CIPs, 33
Code visual aids, 47–48
Communication
  less successful CIPs, 124
  successful CIPs, **11**, 44–47, **61**, 62
Continuous improvement projects
    (CIPs); *see also* case
    studies
  overview, 135–136
  classification, 4–5, 118
  definitions, 3–4
  identification of, 117
  limitations and future work, 141
  managing, 23–24, 26–33
  senior projects as sources of, 23–24
  success defined, 5–6
  success factors, 6–7, 18–19, 103–112,
    138, **139–140**
"Control" phase, 87, 96–98
Critical success factors, 103–112, 138,
    139–140
Cross-functionality, **9**

Current reality trees (CRT), *46*, 59, 137
Customer perceived impact, **6**
Customer satisfaction, 6

D

Daily Floor Management System
    (DFMS), 96
Data
    availability and trustworthiness, **15**,
       120, 129
    historical, 40, 48
    research methodologies, 104–105
"Define" phase, 86, 87–88
Deming's Plan-Do-Check-Act (PDCA),
    4, 55, 57–65, 123
"Design" phase, 47–48, 75–77
DMAIC (Define, Measure, Analyze,
    Improve, and Control), 4, **5**,
    85–98
Documentation, **12**, 70, 74, 75, 76–78, 80;
    see also standard operating
    procedures (SOP)
"Do" phase, 62–64

E

Emergency Medical Services (EMS) *see*
    ambulance response times
"Evaluation" phase, 78–80
Excel, 62, 65, 97
Execution of CIPs, 29–31

F

Facilitation, **15**
Failure, causes of, 58–59, *60*
Final reports, 118
Financial resources, **14**
Follow-up activities, **17**
Food industry *see* material waste reduction
Fulfillment levels *see* order fulfillment
    levels

G

Gemba walks, 88
General Process of System Interventions
    overview, 37–38

analysis phase, 41–46
design and implementation phase,
    47–48
pre-diagnostic phase, 38–41
results phase, 48–52
General quality improvement projects, 4,
    5
Geographic analysis, 137
Global positioning systems (GPS), 48
Goals, 4, **7**, **107**, 120, 128
Goldratt, Eliyahu, 137

H

Hardware organization, 122–125
Health services *see* ambulance
    response times

I

Identification of CIPs, 26–27, 117
"Implement" phase, 47–48, 77–78
"Improve" phase, 87, 92–96
Industrial and Systems Engineering (ISE)
    students *see* university CIPs
Information flows, **61**, 62, 65
Input-process-output diagram, *40*, 136
Institutionalization, **12**
International projects, 24–25
Interviews, 118
Inventory management, 128–130
Ishikawa diagrams, 136–137

J

"Just-do-it" actions, 93, 137

K

Kaizen
    blitz, 93–94
    events, 4, **5**, 94–96, 137
    tools and mechanisms, 3
Kovach, 86

L

Leadership of university CIPs, 30–32
Leakages, 93, 95, 97–98

Lean
 definitions, 85
 projects/events, 4
Lean manufacturing
 "Analyze" phase, 72–75
 "Design" phase, 75–77
 "Evaluation" phase, 78–80
 "Implement" phase, 77–78
 "Plan" phase, 70–72
 "Standardize" phase, 80
Lean Six Sigma
 overview, 4, 85–86
 Analyze phase, 87, 90–92
 Control phase, 87, 96–98
 Define phase, 86, 87–88
 Improve phase, 87, 92–96
 Measure phase, 87, 88–90
 projects, **5**
Lessons learned, **17**
Less successful continuous improvement
  projects (CIPs)
 overview, 115–118, 125–126, 138
 production line stoppages, 118–122
 sale opportunity reduction, 122–125
Location of ambulances, 48

M

Maintenance, 97–98
Management, **13**
Mapping, 136
Material waste reduction
 CIP resume, 85–86
 DMAIC methodology, 86–98
 success factors, 98–101
"Measure" phase, 87, 88–90
Meetings
 less successful CIPs, 124
 material waste reduction, 97
 order fulfillment levels, 62–63
 university CIPs, 30–32, 33
Mexican university CIPs *see*
  university CIPs
Monterrey metropolitan area,
  37–38, 39

N

Non-value added activities, 42–44, 47

O

Operational Production Indicator (OPI),
  69, 72–73, 78–80
Optimization models, 69–70, 76,
  77–80, 137
Order fulfillment levels
 CIP resume, 55–56
 Plan-Do-Check-Act (PDCA), 57–65
 resources needed, 56–57
 success factors, 65–68
Organization factors, **13–17**, **140**
Overall Equipment Effectiveness
  (OEE), 69

P

Packaging, 88, 89–90, 93–94, 95–96;
  see also setup time in a
  packaging line
Paramedic response time, 38–39, 40,
  42–43
Pareto diagrams, *60*, 90, *91*
Perceptions of success factors
 ambulance response times, 50–52
 less successful CIPs, 121–122,
  124–125
 material waste reduction, 99–101
 most important factors, 107–109
 order fulfillment levels, 67–68
 production line stoppages, 80–83
 university CIPs, **33–34**
 unsuccessful CIPs, 129–130, 131–132
Performance evaluation/review, **16**
Performance metrics
 overview, 5–6
 ambulance response times, 37, 38–39,
  40–41
 Operational Production Indicator
  (OPI), 69, 72–73, 78–80
 order fulfillment levels, 55
 sale opportunity, 122–123
Plan-Do-Check-Act (PDCA), 4, 55,
  57–65, 123
Plan-Do-Study-Act (PDSA), 4
"Plan" phase, 57–62, 70–72
Pre-diagnostic phase, 38–41
Prioritizing, **14**
Problem scopes, **8**

Problem-solving methodologies
    Deming's Plan-Do-Check-Act
        (PDCA), 55, 57–65, 123
    DMAIC (Define, Measure, Analyze,
        Improve, and Control), 85–98
    General Process of System
        Interventions, 38–52
    Lean, 70–80
    seven-steps process improvement, 119
    types of, 4
Process factors, **11–12**, **139–140**
Process improvement projects, 4, **5**
Process standardization, 59, **61**, 93, 95
Product identification labels, 63, 65
Production line stoppages, 118–122
Production sequences, 75–76, 77, 78–79
Progress reporting, **12**
Projects
    identification and selection, **13**
    scope of, **8**, 123, 129

Q

Quality circles, 4–5
Quality improvement projects, 4, **5**

R

Radio operators, 40, **43**, **45–46**, 47
Rapid improvement events, 4
Raw materials
    production line stoppages, 74
    requisitions, *64*
    waste reduction, 88, 89, 90–91, 93, 95
Recognition and rewards, **15–16**
Record keeping, 89
Research methodologies, 103–105, 112
Research projects, 25
Resources needed, **14**, 56–57
"Results" phase, 48–52
Rich pictures, *56*, 136

S

Sale opportunity reduction, 122–125
Sampling, 88, 104
Semi-finished products, 88, 90–91, 93–95
Senior projects, 24–26; *see also*
    university CIPs

Setup time in a packaging line
    CIP resume, 69–70
    lean manufacturing, 70–80
    success factors, 80–83
Seven-steps Process Improvement
    Problem-Solving
    Methodology, 119
SIPOC diagram, *89*, 136
Six Sigma projects, 4, **5**, 85; *see also*
    DMAIC (Define, Measure,
    Analyze, Improve, and
    Control)
Software, **15**
Solution iterations, **12**
Sources of CIPs, 24–26
Sponsors, **10**
Spreadsheets, 62, 65, 97
Stakeholder representation, **9**
"Standardize" phase, 80
Standard operating procedures (SOP),
    74, 76–77, 93, 98
Stock keeping units (SKUs), 73, 75, 76, 79,
    80, 90, 97
Storage, 118–122
Structured methodology, **11**
Success factors
    overview, 6–7, 18–19
    case study: ambulance response
        times, 49–50
    case study: material waste
        reduction, 98–101
    case study: order fulfillment levels,
        65–68
    case study: setup time in a packaging
        line, 80–83
    critical factors, 103–112, 138, **139–140**
    lack of, 121–122, 124–125, 129–130
    organization factors, **13–17**, **140**
    perceptions of, 33–34, 107–109
    process factors, **11–12**, **139–140**
    research methodologies, 103–107
    task design factors, 7–**8**, **139**
    team design factors, **9–10**, **139**
Successful continuous improvement
    projects (CIPs)
    overview, 35–36, 136–137
    ambulance response times, 37–52
    critical success factors, 103–112

definitions, 5–6
material waste reduction, 85–101
order fulfillment levels, 55–68
setup time in a packaging line,
    69–83
Supplier-input-process-output-
    customer (SIPOC)
    diagram, *89*, 136
Support
    from continuous improvement
        program, **17**
    from management, **13**
Surveys, 106–107, 118
System thinking, 136

T

Target areas
    commitment to change, **8**, 18, 107, **139**
    representation, 131
    task design factors, **8**
    team design factors, **10**
Task design factors, **7–8**, **139**
Team design factors, **9–10**, **139**
Teams
    improvement skills, 120, 129
    membership of, 123–124, 129, 131
    perceptions of success, **33–34**, 50–52
    university CIPs, 25
Technical documentation, **12**
Timeframes, **8**, 23, 32
Tool appropriateness, **11**, 129
Training, **15**
Transportation costs, 130–132

Travelling Salesman Problem, 70
Turtle diagrams, *57*, 136

U

University CIPs
    overview, 23–24
    CIP approval, 27–29
    CIP assessment, 31–32
    CIP closing, 33
    CIP execution, 29–31
    CIP identification, 26–27
    perceptions of success factors,
        33–34
    senior projects as source of,
        24–26
Unsuccessful continuous
    improvement projects
    (CIPs), 127–132, 133, 138

V

Valid responses, 105–107
Visual aids, 47–48, 70, 77, 78, *79*

W

Warehouse controls, **61**, 63
Waste reduction
    CIP resume, 85–86
    DMAIC methodology, 86–98
    success factors, 98–101
Wire and cable company *see* order
    fulfillment levels

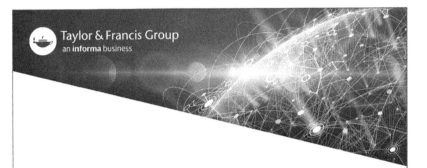